The History and Economics of the New Hampshire Dairy Industry

"Let us not forget that the cultivation of the earth is the most important labor of man. When tillage begins other arts will follow. The farmers therefore are the founders of civilization."

Daniel Webster

Table of Contents

Dedication 4

Acknowledgements 5

New Hampshire Dairy Hall of Fame 7

New Hampshire Dairy Industry History 9

State Government's Role in the Development of the NH Dairy Industry 25

The New Hampshire Dairy Industry 35

Producer-Distributors 39

Commercial Processors 47

Milk Marketing 51

Quality of Life, Agritourism and Ecological Value 71

Wildlife and Grassland Habitats 81

Economic Model 85

The Cost of Producing Milk on New Hampshire Dairy Farms 93

The University of New Hampshire and the State's Dairy Industry 101

The Future of New Hampshire's Dairy Industry 105

References 108

Appendix 114

Dedication

This book is dedicated to Ernest A. (Ernie) George and Kevin B. Kennedy. They were area dairy specialists who advised dairy producers around New Hampshire during those rapidly changing years in the industry from the 1950s to the 1980s. They served as mentors to several of us involved with the writing of this book, who currently work with UNH Cooperative Extension.

Ernest (Ernie) George

Ernie grew up in New Hampshire and lived throughout central and southern regions as his father managed several institutional dairy herds.

Ernie graduated from UNH in 1951 with a B.S. degree in Dairy Husbandry and a minor in Animal Science. He served as a meat inspector in the U.S. Army in the early 1950s in the Boston area.

Following his Army service he worked for Massachusetts Extension, Worcester County, as a dairy specialist. In 1955 he began work for UNH Cooperative Extension as the Hillsborough County Agricultural Agent and Southern New Hampshire Regional Dairy Specialist. He retired from UNH Cooperative Extension in 1985 after 30 years of service. Ernie was well known for his extensive milk bottle collection.

Ernest A. George

Ernie involved his family in his professional life, including his wife of 47 years, Arlene Bailey George, and his children Larry George, Carol George Farley, Susan George Cummings and Jim George. Ernie passed away in 1998.

Kevin B. Kennedy

Kevin, born in Bruno, Saskatchewan, served with the British Fleet Air Arm during World War II. After graduating from the Ontario Agricultural College in 1949, he was employed as a sales trainee for International Harvestor Company of Canada. From 1951-1955, he was a technician with the New Hampshire-Vermont Breeding Association serving in the Keene area. Kevin was always proud of his Canadian heritage, but it was the dairy industry of New Hampshire that Kevin served for more than 30 years.

Kevin B. Kennedy

In 1955, Kevin joined UNH Cooperative Extension as Assistant County Agricultural Agent for Grafton County. In 1966, he was appointed as Area Dairy Agent for Cheshire, Grafton and Sullivan counties. His position after 1972 was Area Dairy Agent for Grafton and Coos Counties.

Kevin's family was very dear to him and included his wife of 35 years, Joan and his nine children: Brian Kennedy, Brenda Robb, Susan Kennedy, Maureen Fuller, Kevin Kennedy, Kathryn Robito, Michael Kennedy, John Kennedy and Claire Touseau. Kevin served with UNH Cooperative Extension until his death in 1983.

Acknowledgements

Authors

This book brings together the collective expertise of several UNH Cooperative Extension specialists and educators and other dairy industry and agency people. Authors include:

Peter Erickson, Ph.D., Extension Specialist, Dairy and Associate Professor, Animal and Nutritional Sciences (University of New Hampshire section)

Francis E. Gilman, Extension Agricultural Engineer, Emeritus
(Contributed to the Dairy History section)

Michal Lunak, Ph.D., Extension Assistant Professor/Specialist, Dairy
(Economic Model section)

Lorraine Stuart Merrill, Commissioner, NH Dept. of Agriculture, Markets & Foods, partner in Stuart Farm, and freelance writer
(State Government's Role in NH Dairy section)

John C. Porter, Extension Professor/Specialist, Emeritus, Dairy
(History, Dairy Industry, Producer-Distributor, Commercial Processors, Ecological Value, Future of NH Dairy sections and over-all editor)

Christine Braley Rasmussen, Executor Director of New England Family Dairy Farms Cooperative (Milk Marketing section)

Michael Sciabarrasi, Extension Professor/Specialist, Agricultural Business Management
(Cost of Production section)

Matthew Tarr, Extension Specialist, Wildlife (Wildlife section)

Dorothy Taylor, Director of the Center for Land Conservation Assistance at the Society for the Protection of New Hampshire Forests (Quality of Life and Open Space sections)

Stephen Taylor, former Commissioner, NH Dept. of Agriculture, Markets & Food (State Government's Role in NH Dairy section)

New England Family Dairy Farms Cooperative (NEFDFC)

The New England Family Dairy Farms Cooperative (NEFDFC) identified a need for a publication that would assist them in educating citizens regarding the financial difficulties facing farmers in New Hampshire as well as much of New England. Members of NEFDFC believe that, if left unchecked, these difficulties may result in farmland disappearing from New England in the next fifteen to twenty years. Their hope was that if citizens receive information about the significant amenities that farms contribute to the New England region, for which they currently receive little if any compensation, people would be willing to pay an increased amount for local products, including milk. If people purchased local products for a price that approaches more closely the cost of production, farmers could continue to contribute to maintaining green space, ag-related jobs, wildlife habitat, historical resources, and the community character that attracts both visitors and residents to New Hampshire.

Photography

Unless otherwise noted, the photography work was done by John Porter and the old photos are from his archive collection.

Granite State Dairy Promotion (GSDP)

In response to the initiative from NEFDFC, Granite State Dairy Promotion provided major financial support to UNH Cooperative Extension to conduct a study about the New Hampshire dairy industry.

Graphics and Design

Karen Busch Holman, a graphic designer from East Andover, created the layout and design. Gillian Hodges Rapp and Mary West, Merrimack County UNH Cooperative Extension Administrative Assistants, did the word processing and photo scanning. UNH Printing Services provided color scans and the final printing of the book.

Technical Review and Copy Editing

This book was edited by James Garvin, State Architectural Historian; Gail McWilliam Jellie, Director of Agricultural Promotion, NH Department of Agriculture, Markets & Food; Rob Johnson, Executive Director, NH Farm Bureau Federation; Martha Porter, wife of one of the authors; Steve Taylor, former Commissioner, Department of Agriculture, Markets & Food, and Christine Braley Rasmussen, Executive Director of NEFDFC. Holly Young, UNH Educational Marketing & Information Coordinator, helped in the final editing and publishing of the work in conjunction with UNH Printing Services, and Peg Boyles, UNH Cooperative Extension Writer/Editor provided technical review and copy editing services.

Special Thanks

A special thanks to Dr. Judith Moyer for granting permission to extensively reference her article, "From Dairy to Doorstep;" Historic New England, Historical Society of Cheshire County, HP Hood and the NH Historical Society for permission to reprint selected photography.

Thanks to Dave Mikelson, statistician for the New England Field Office of the National Agricultural Statistics Service, for spending time to research archival data from the United States Census office and for collecting and organizing information from the New England Agricultural Statistics Service. Also, thanks to Robert Cottrell, Director of the Remick Farm Museum in Tamworth, for supplying some historical articles and time-line facts about the New Hampshire dairy industry. Robert D. Wellington, Sr., Vice President and Chief Economist for Agri-Mark Dairy Cooperative reviewed the Milk Marketing section.

Financial Support

Granite State Dairy Promotion provided major financial support for this book. Color printing was made possible by the support of the Andrew C. and Margaret R. Sigler Foundation.

New Hampshire Dairy Hall of Fame

The picture below captures some key players in the New Hampshire dairy industry known to many at the time this book was printed. They were recognized leaders who were instrumental in influencing the dairy industry during its years of rapid change.

Left to right: Dr. Tom Fairchild, Extension Dairyman and later chair of the Department of Animal and Nutritional Sciences, Dean of the College of Life Sciences and Agriculture and interim University president; Richard Rutherford, long-time agricultural agent in Grafton County; George Clement, well-known dairyman and auctioneer from Landaff; Dr. James Holter, nationally known ruminant nutritionist from UNH; Roe McDanolds, a highly respected dairyman from North Haverhill; Kevin Kennedy, long-time area dairy specialist from Grafton County; and Dr. Hilton Boynton, internationally-known dairy specialist and cattle judge. (Fred Beane, Manchester Union Sunday news photo, circa 1970, provided by Brenda Kennedy Robb.)

Hay raked into cocks for drying before loaded onto wagons, circa 1930s - 1940s.

New Hampshire Dairy Industry History

The earliest information about dairying in New Hampshire is in a letter written August 6, 1634, by Mr. Ambrose Gibbons, manager of Captain John Mason's plantation, which encompassed the present city of Portsmouth. In the letter to his employer he itemized the number of head of dairy cows he was managing and his need for a husband and wife team to help make butter and cheese. These cattle were said to have been a "yellow" breed from Denmark, and their progeny formed the foundation stock of the early settlers in many New England colonies (Weld, 1905, p. 71).

Similar to other New England states, New Hampshire's dairy industry started as a subsistence form of farming. The state's earliest settlers established homesteads on the hillsides where there were nice breezes in the summer, heavy soils, protection from flooding and good views (Porter, 1985, p.1). They raised food for their own use and for barter. Dairy cattle were found on nearly all of these early farms to supply milk and dairy products to the family. Most old barns in New Hampshire were originally built to house animals and store feed. Since dairy cattle were found on nearly all farms, it became the responsibility of the women to make cheese and butter from the excess supplies of milk. Whey from cheese-making and extra milk was fed to the pigs. These milk products provided ways to store food without refrigeration.

As milk production increased with the growth in animal numbers on each farm, and the number of people living in villages grew, there was a need to market milk and other farm products from the country to the city. Individual farms sold milk and cream in nearby towns and cities in the 19th century (Moyer, 2003, p. 101). In the 1800s, the principal breeds of livestock were Durham and Ayrshire cattle, Merino sheep, and the newly-developed Morgan horse (U.S. Soil Conservation Service, 1976. p.6).

Dairying has been one of the principal sectors of New Hampshire agriculture for many years. As stated in the 1905 University of New Hampshire Extension Bulletin No. 120, "Unlike other branches of agriculture, dairying does not rob the soil of its fertility. Dairying is a self supporting industry and not dependent on the artificial. It is therefore an ideal industry, because from its own resources it is able to sustain itself forever," (Weld, 1905, p. 73).

New Hampshire conditions seemed favorable to dairying. In 1917, Extension Bulletin No. 8 stated:

> Of the natural advantages which favor dairying in New Hampshire is the success with which hay and forage crops can be grown. The soils generally seed readily, grass, timothy and clover the principal grasses grown. A volunteer grass (witch grass) is cut for hay in some places, but is generally regarded as a pest. Leguminous crops can be grown and more attention is being given to them. In some of the counties the soybean is gaining favor, and this plant forms one of the important cover crops. Corn is the most important grain crop. Much of the rougher lands in the state can be used for pasture, and when properly stocked and cared for, six to nine acres are required per cow (Davis, 1917, pp. 9 -10).

New Hampshire's geography was important in shaping its destiny. The river system provided water power for mills and caused the industrial sector to expand, bringing workers and their families who needed food to the area. The plenteous rainfall and green pastures made a good environment for dairy farming (Moyer, 2003, p. 101). This is evidenced by the extensive stonewalls that were built as fences around the edges of fields cleared for pastures and crop production. Old Yankee barns were used to house dairy and livestock animals, and many were built in the 1850-1865 time period and still stand today. Yankee barns have large doors located on their gable ends, which were more practical than the earlier English barns with doors located on the side under the eaves (Porter and Gilman, 2001, p. 11).

Railroad

Another advantage to the dairy industry was its proximity to Boston. Milk began traveling by rail to distant markets such as Boston in the 1840s. Harvey Perley Hood (1823-1900) of Derry was one of the first farmers in southern New Hampshire to supply the Boston market. He built a creamery in Derry and shipped butter to Boston. About 1844, HP Hood bought a milk route in Charlestown, MA and began shipping milk in cans to Boston. Ten years later he formed the HP Hood company, which grew into one of the largest dairy processors in New England, developing a loyal customer base as a recognized New England brand (Moyer, 2003, p. 101).

Farmers near railroads benefited the most from the Boston market. The railroad allowed agricultural products to be shipped further away from the farm and opened new markets. Milk can platforms were beside the railroad tracks where area farmers would leave their milk. At one point, it was said there were 147 railway stations in New Hampshire from which milk was forwarded to Boston six days a week (Weld, 1905, p. 76).

Civil War

The period around the Civil War was the heyday of New Hampshire agriculture, as was the case throughout the entire country. As Isaac Newton, U.S. Secretary of Agriculture stated:

Musterfield Farm, Sutton

> While more than a million of the hardy sons of toil have been called from their industrial pursuits to engage in warfare for the preservation of the Union, those at home have applied themselves with redoubled energy; and with the influence of higher wages in calling forth economizing labor and the aid of agricultural machinery and labor-saving implements and appliances, the farmer has been enabled to gather an abundant harvest (Newton, 1865, p. 1).

The Civil War Era was a turning point in the development of commercial agriculture, as well as the growth of industrialization.

Land Grant System

Agriculture continued to flourish in the 1800s. Recognizing the value of education in strengthening the United States in the war-torn era, Justin Morrill, a U.S. Representative from Vermont, worked to enact the Morrill Land Grant Act, signed by Abraham Lincoln in 1862. This gave 30,000 acres of federal land to each member of Congress, which could be used as a site for an agricultural and mechanical arts college. The sale of some of the land could be used to establish a college that would offer courses in agricultural engineering, production practices, home economics and academics; however, each state had to provide the budget for general operation and maintenance. This was done to avoid "extravagance in the external management of their affairs and especially by indulgence in architectural display," (French, 1865, p. 140). Congress didn't want money invested in lavish buildings, but rather in a practical education affordable by rural citizens.

The New Hampshire College of Agriculture and Mechanic Arts got its start in Hanover as a result of legislation in 1866. The College settled in Durham in 1893 on land willed to the state for that purpose by Benjamin Thompson, a progressive Durham farmer. In 1923 the name was changed to the University of New Hampshire and the campus continues to grow and support its mission today (U.S. Soil Conservation Service, 1976, p 15).

Granite State Dairymen Association

The railroad was an important factor in the early growth of New Hampshire's dairy industry, and rail rates, pick-up points and rights-of-way were often a point of discussion among farmers. On February 26, 1884 a meeting was called at the City Hotel in Manchester, "…to effect an organization in the interest of dairying," (Granite State Dairymen, 1884, pp. 5 -17). The motivator behind this was James M. Connor of Hopkinton, a successful butter maker, who sought to improve the marketing of dairy products and use the railroad distribution system.

University of New Hampshire, circa 1930s.

On March 18, 1884, the constitution and by-laws were enacted for the Granite State Dairymen's Association and Connor was elected the first president. Records of the Association indicated that their early meetings revolved around techniques for making quality butter, new technology for separating cream from milk and regulating the sale of "oleomargarine."

Granite State Dairymen was a very influential organization in its day. Towns used to bid to host its annual meeting because it brought so many people to the area. A notation in the minutes in Lisbon on December 8, 1906 states, "The attendance at the session was estimated as follows: morning 300, afternoon 500, evening 700. It was generally conceded to be the most largely attended and most valuable meeting in the history of the association," (Granite State Dairymen, 1906, p. 205). This organization continued to work for the New Hampshire dairy industry over the years and was one of the oldest dairy organizations in the United States when it dissolved in 1998, due to lack of membership and the establishment of other organizations that were able to serve the needs of the industry. Granite State Dairymen championed many causes including:

- Appropriations from the state for butter tests to evaluate methods of cream separation and awards for state and regional dairy product exhibitions.

- Resolution for constructing a dairy building at UNH in 1909.

- A resolution opposing the change of NH College of Agriculture and Mechanic Arts to the University of New Hampshire in 1911.

- State support of testing herds for tuberculosis in 1933.

- Formation of the State Milk Control Board in 1935.

- Establishment of a state artificial breeding association in 1945.

- State support of Bangs eradication and herd testing at least twice a year in 1947.

- Continuation and promotion of the Green Pastures Program in 1948.

- Maintaining the New Hampshire Milk Control Board in 1963.

- The Dairy Compact concept in 1993.

    (Source - Granite State Dairymen Association minutes).

Butter and Cheese Production

U.S. Agricultural Census information on the New Hampshire dairy industry can be traced back to 1850. Prior to 1856, butter-making was strictly a farm operation. To make butter, it is necessary to separate the cream from the milk and that arduous task was made easier by technological developments. In 1856 the first small creamery and cheese factory in the country was started in Orange County, New York, and it wasn't until 1871 that the first, large, commercial creamery for making butter was built in Iowa (Judkins and Keener, 1960, p. 334). New Hampshire had its early entrepreneurs in the dairy processing business. The first private creamery business in New Hampshire was constructed by Charles H. Waterhouse in the town of Barrington in 1881. He was also the manager of the first cooperative creamery established by dairy farmers in New Hampshire, located in the Suncook Valley at Short Falls in the town of Epsom. Richard B. Ball of North Monroe was the owner of the first centrifugal cream separator used in the state, having purchased a commercial size machine in 1884. The Hanover creamery in Hanover was the first cooperative in the state to use power machines to separate cream (Weld, 1905, p. 72).

"Creamery" was the term used to denote a specialized processing plant that produced butter. At the height of the industry there were 52 creameries in 44 different towns in New Hampshire (Weld, 1905, p.75). This emphasis on butter production reflects the way dairy production was reported. In fact, fluid milk wasn't initially a major commodity in the state and it took the Census until 1880 before milk was added to the butter and cheese statistics.

Although not known for large volumes of cheese production, New Hampshire had several cheese factories in the early 1900s including:

- Bear Rock Cheese Factory – Stewartstown
- Cedar Brook Cheese Factory – Stewartstown
- Clarksville Cheese Factory – Clarksville
- Columbia Cheese Factory – East Columbia
- Contoocook Greek Cheese Factory – Contoocook
- Dunbarton Greek Cheese Factory – Dunbarton
- East Colebrook Cheese Factory – East Colebrook
- Greek Cheese Factory - Woodsville
- Hood's Cheese Factory – South Lancaster
- Mohawk Dairy Company – Pittsburg
- Valley Brook and Percy Stream Factory – Pittsburg

(Davis, 1917, p. 36; Weld, 1905, p.75).

Fluid Milk

Around 1900, the development of oleomargarine was a threat to the butter industry. This was a butter substitute made from vegetable oils or animal fats. With the drop in butter sales, the New Hampshire dairy industry started a decline from which it never recovered. Even the State Board of Agriculture, seeing the reduction in farming operations, published a promotional booklet entitled, "New Hampshire Farms for Summer Homes." In this they promoted the availability of farms in each county for adaptation to summer home purposes (Bachelder, 1909, p. 5).

In the 1920s there was a shift from creameries making butter to farm processing plants bottling milk. The growing urban population had a need for fresh fluid milk delivered to their doorstep and this market helped replace some of the declining butter sales. Richard Clark, a noted milk bottle collector in Bedford, NH, has over 918 different New Hampshire bottles in his collection. Since some farms marketed under multiple names, it's safe to say that there were between 800-900 dairies marketing bottled milk (Clark, 2006).

Milk Production Data

Table 1 summarizes the New Hampshire dairy industry from 1850-2006. There were a lot of variations in the way data was reported from year to year. Sometimes all farms with dairy animals were recorded and other times only farms that generated their major source of income from dairy products. Milk was reported in pounds and gallons and sometimes only as cheese or butter products. An attempt has been made to report all dairy products on a milk-pounds equivalent basis to make comparisons easier. These calculations were based on the following conversion factors:

Typical image of New Hampshire's landscape in the early 1800s.

Product	Pounds of raw milk to make 1 pound of product
Butter	21.91
Cheese	9.23

Assumed milk to weigh 8.6 lbs / gallon (Source: Adams et al., 1995, p. 228)

Table 1. Dairy Farm Numbers and Production from 1850-2006

Year	Number of Dairy Farms	Number of Milking Cows	Milk Produced Per Cow/Year	Total Annual Milk Production (million lbs)
1850	N.A. *	94,277 [a]	N.A.	182 [c]
1860	N.A.	94,880 [a]	N.A.	173 [c]
1870	N.A.	90,583 [a]	N.A.	159 [d]
1880	N.A.	90,564 [a]	N.A.	216 [e]
1890	N.A.	109,423 [a]	N.A.	367 [f]
1900	22,519 [a]; 9,788 [j]	115,036 [a]	N.A.	522 [g]
1910	20,168 [a]	81,561 [a]	N.A.	454 [h]
1920	15,925 [a]	95,997 [a]	N.A.	N.A.
1925	14,798 [a]	81,504 [a] 79,000 [b]	4,980 [b]	393 [b]
1930	11,018 [a]	68,792 [a] 75,000 [b]	5,090 [b]	382 [b]
1940	10,572 [a]	73,000 [b]	4,940 [b]	361 [b]
1950	7,585 [a]	61,000 [b]	5,640 [b]	344 [b]
1960	3,587 [a]; 2,700 [k]	51,000 [b]	7,660 [b]	391 [b]
1970	1,300 [i]; 820 [k]	36,000 [b]	9,889 [b]	356 [b]
1980	900 [i]; 505 [k]	30,000 [b]	11,567 [b]	347 [b]
1990	400 [i]; 274 [k]	20,000 [b]	15,100 [b]	302 [b]
1995	400 [i]; 241 [k]	20,000 [b]	16,300 [b]	326 [b]
2000	270 [i]; 181 [k]	18,000 [b]	17,333 [b]	312 [b]
2004	210 [i] 140 [k]	16,000 [b]	18,938 [b]	303 [b]
2005	200 [i] 140 [k]	16,000 [b]	18,875 [b]	302 [b]
2006	200 [i] 130 [k]	15,000 [b]	19,533 [b]	293 [b]

*N.A. – not available

a. U.S. Census of Agriculture, 1925, 1930, 1940, 1950 Volume II, and 1959, all farms producing milk.

b. National Agricultural Statistics Service, 1925-2006. Milk Production, Disposition and Income Annual Summaries.

c. U.S. Census of Agriculture, milk pounds equivalent calculated from pounds of butter and cheese produced.

d. U.S. Census of Agriculture, milk pounds equivalent calculated from gallons of milk sold and pounds of butter and cheese product produced.

e. U.S. Census of Agriculture, milk pounds equivalent calculated from gallons of milk sold or sent to butter and cheese factories and pounds of butter and cheese made on farms.

f. U.S. Census of Agriculture, milk pounds equivalent calculated from gallons of all milk produced on the farm.

g. U.S. Census of Agriculture, milk pounds equivalent calculated from total gallons of milk produced.

h. U.S. Census of Agriculture, calculated from gallons of milk/cow/year and milk equivalent from butter and cheese (Davis, 1917, p. 8).

i. National Agriculture Statistics Service (NASS) all farms reporting dairy cows.

j. U.S. Census of Agriculture, 1900, farms deriving 40% or more of income from dairy products.

k. Number of farms with permits for commercial shipping of milk from the division of Public Health and Human Services, Dairy Division, adjusted to include only commercial dairy farmers.

Modern Era

After World War II, dairy farms started to change from the prevalent 10-20 cows per herd to 40 or more milking animals per farm. This was due to new developments such as the wider availability of electricity to run milking machines, tractors, hay balers, mechanical barn cleaners, etc. Changes in the dairy sanitation laws requiring cows to be milked on concrete caused several farms to move their milking herds from second-floor wooden stables to barn basements with concrete floors. This is evidenced in many barns with whitewash, required for sanitizing milking barns, residual on the walls of upstairs hay mows.

During this time, Yankee-style barns were expanded by putting ceilings over the hayloft side of the barn, adding another row of cows. One-story additions were also extended to the ends of old barns to increase their capacity. Generally cows were hitched in rigid stanchions and later comfort stalls, which secured the cows with a neck-chain on a rail, allowing more movement. The cows were milked in their assigned stalls.

Dairy cows tied by their neck in most of our fine old post and beam barns often never stepped out of their stalls from mid-October to mid-May. UNH herdsman Ken Fowler wrote in 1947, that cow comfort should be given more consideration in barn planning. The University of New Hampshire started using a form of dairy cattle loose-housing called pen-barns in 1932. Four breeds of dairy cows were separated into groups by breed in bedded pens that were cleaned daily. This was a radical change in housing using purebred animals, which were considered best of their breed worldwide. These pens were warm like most stanchion barns, meaning temperatures were usually kept at about 50 degrees or at least above freezing. Other terms for group-pen housing were loafing, cafeteria style and free-run barns.

By October 31, 1950, Cornell graduate Ivan Bigelow, a district agricultural engineer in New York that majored in barn planning and construction, was pioneering the use of one-story pole-barns and loose dairy cattle housing. In 1953, the Charles H. Hood Foundation hired Bigelow as a consultant for dairy farmers to assist with housing problems. He particularly focused on this newly-developed concept of loose-housing and pen-stables. At the same time, milk handling and transportation changed from individual, ten-gallon can containers cooled in refrigerated water tanks to bulk refrigerated tanks and bulk tank truck transportation to processing plants, lending itself to larger dairy operations.

Cattle in loose-housing had a feeding area, a resting area and a separate milking area soon to be called a "milking parlor." Cows moved on their own to each of these areas, eating and drinking by choice. They were gathered in a holding area prior to entering the milking stalls that were raised so that the milker could stand upright while prepping and attaching the milking units easily to the cow's udder. Prior to this, farmers had to carry feed and sometimes water to each cow, clean the manure from behind the cows at least twice a day and partially crawl under each cow to milk. The early loose-housing rest areas became known as "bedded-packs" and manure was removed once or twice a year. These were often poorly maintained; however, they could work well if managed correctly and had the advantage of built-in manure storage.

In 1960, an enterprising Washington State dairyman discovered that given the opportunity, cows would voluntarily use "free-stalls" for resting. These were bedded stalls approximately the same dimensions as confined cow-barn stalls, but with no restraints. Amazingly, most cows quickly and on their own, chose the comfort offered by these open stalls for resting.

Harold Bodwell in Kensington, NH, was the first farmer in the state to convert his bedded-pack system for 54 cows to free-stalls. By the end of 1963, there were six installations in New Hampshire and by December 31, 1964, 33 in or under construction.

Ivan Bigelow, of the Hood Foundation, was replaced by Rodney Martin in 1955, who became well-known for encouraging dairy producers in the Northeast to abandon old, inefficient facilities and replace them with new ones. Groups like the Dairy Practices Council wrote guidelines for constructing these new facilities and worked in conjunction with Cooperative Extension throughout the country to get these new ideas out to dairy producers. This type of dairy housing led to a huge reduction in hand labor, making it possible for one person to care for many more cows. Most of these installations were cold housing in open-front, south-facing buildings in the Northeastern states. From 1957 to 1964, Hood designed about 140 systems in New York and New England. Initially, it was felt that only a few breeds, mainly Holsteins, should be in cold housing in the Northeastern States. Ultimately, most breeds adjusted well with improved herd health.

After a few years with the Hood Foundation, Rod Martin was transferred to the HP Hood Dairy Farm Engineering Service and then went on to do similar work with Agway, followed up by Stanley Weeks, who continues to consult in New Hampshire. Today new technology continues to be carried to New Hampshire dairy producers by UNH Cooperative Extension, consultants and company representatives. Innovations such as greenhouse and fabric-covered barns, composted bedded-packs and robotic milking provide a variety of options for New Hampshire dairy producers to operate efficient farms.

Time Line

As the dairy industry in New Hampshire matured, many changes occurred and new challenges emerged with each passing decade:

1840s-1860s

- The change from hand power and oxen to horses started the American agricultural revolution.
- The first rail shipment occured in 1851.
- Ayrshire, Jersey and Holstein cattle were imported and bred.
- The first milk laws were passed in Boston in 1856, making it illegal to add water or remove cream from milk.
- Gail Borden received a patent for the first successful milk condensing plant in 1856.
- Louis Pasteur developed the process of heating milk to kill bacteria in 1864.
- Civil War introduced New Hampshire men to new land resources and the farm exodus began.
- The first vacuum-type milking machine was patented in 1865.
- New Hampshire College of Agriculture and Mechanic Arts opened in Hanover in 1866.

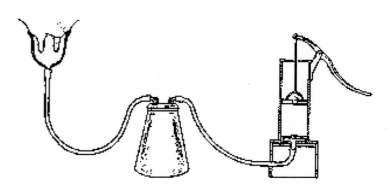

Hodges and Brockendon milking machine from England, 1851. Source Milking Systems and Milk Management (NRAES – 26).

1870s

- The railroad boom broadened agricultural markets.
- Silos came into use for storing fermented forage crops.

1880s

- Granite State Dairymen's Association was established in 1884.
- The glass milk bottle was invented in 1884.
- The depressed wool and meat industries created interest in developing the dairy industry in the state.
- The dairy industry became concerned about western agriculture competing against the northeast.
- Cattle breeding and crossbreeding were becoming of more interest as a means to influence the butterfat content of the milk.
- A bottle filler machine was invented in 1886.
- The Hatch Act created the first agricultural experiment stations.

1890s

- The development of new milk separating machines which were more efficient in removing cream for making butter.
- The first gasoline powered tractor was invented.
- The Meat Inspection Act of 1890 established USDA inspectors to enforce sanitary standards in the meat and dairy industries.
- Balanced dairy rations were promoted at dairy meetings in the 1890s.
- W.D. Hoard, former governor of Wisconsin and editor of the Hoard's Dairyman magazine, spoke at Granite State Dairymen's meetings in 1891, 1893, and 1894 about current dairy production practices.
- The Babcock Test was invented by Stephen Babcock in 1890 and became an acceptable laboratory test to measure for butterfat in milk.
- The New Hampshire College of Agriculture and Mechanic Arts settled in Durham on the land willed by Benjamin Thompson in 1893.
- Pasteurization machines were introduced in the United States in 1895 after being developed by Louis Pasteur in 1864.

1900s

- The devopment of oleomargarine, made from vegetable oils or animal fats, was a threat to butter sales.
- There was the concern about the possible spread of foot and mouth disease from foreign countries.
- The number of cows in the state peaked at 115,036 in 1900.

A tractor demonstration at G.H. Clarke Farm, Boscawen, NH, 1916

1910s

- New Hampshire's dairy industry fell on hard times and production of butter declined.
- For the first time figures showed that more of New Hampshire's population lived in urban rather than rural areas.
- The New Hampshire Department of Agriculture was established in 1913.
- Sullivan County Farmers' Association started in 1913 which led to the N.H. County Farmers' Association and it adopted the Farm Bureau name in 1924.
- Cooperative Extension started as a joint effort with Sullivan County Farmers' Association (Farm Bureau) and became an off-campus outreach of the College in Durham in 1915, bringing research-based information to farmers.
- There was an increased use of commercial fertilizer in growing crops.
- Cow numbers in New Hampshire declined to 81,561.
- The Delaval Milker became the first widely used milking machine in 1918.
- Homogenized milk was sold for the first time in Connecticut 1919.

Cooperative Extension started as a joint effort with Sullivan County Farmers' Association (Farm Bureau). Left to right: M. Gale Eastman, first county agent in New Hampshire, J. Daniel Porter, first Sullivan County Farm Bureau President, and N.H. Wells, Sullivan County Agricultural Agent.

1920s

- There was a shift from creameries making butter and cheese to farm processing plants bottling fluid milk.
- A rapid expansion of local milk processing plants in towns around the state made fresh, fluid milk available to households.
- The New Hampshire College of Agriculture and Mechanic Arts became the University of New Hampshire in 1923.
- The first commercial production of hybrid seed corn occurred in 1926.

1930s

- T.B. and brucellosis outbreaks required the slaughter of many animals and the introduction of vaccination programs.
- All-purpose, rubber tired tractors with complementary machinery were popularized.
- Wax-coated paper milk containers were introduced in 1932.

- The Agricultural Adjustment Act of 1933 established the "Triple A," which was charged with the balance of supply and demand of farm goods. This was the predecessor of the Agricultural Stabilization and Conservation Service (ASCS), which is now the Farm Service Agency (FSA).
- The Soil Erosion Service (SES) was established to show farmers how to protect their land and was also part of the 1933 Act. This was the beginning of the Soil Conservation Service (SCS) which later became Natural Resources Conservation Service (NRCS).
- The Agricultural Marketing Agreement Act authorized Federal Milk Marketing Orders in 1937.

(Soil Conservation Service photo)

Farm conservation plans were used by farmers to control erosion.

1940s

- Electricity became more available in New Hampshire through rural electrification programs and refrigeration proliferated.
- Home refrigeration started a decline in the need for daily delivery of milk.
- The N.H. Artificial Breeding Association was established in 1945.
- The Agricultural Act of 1949 authorized the dairy support program, which still functions today by establishing a floor price for dairy products.

1950s

- Bulk tanks replaced milk cans. Many small producers were forced out when they couldn't afford the cost of a tank. This caused a major shift in the industry.
- Public health requirements required cows to be milked on concrete floors rather than wood.
- Improved highways made milk more transportable across the region.
- Artificial insemination of cows was more widely used and greatly improved genetics and milk production per cow.

1960s

- The introduction of the free-stall and milking parlor concept of dairy cattle management changed the way cows were managed.
- A major change in the state control of the pricing of milk with the dissolution of the NH Milk Control Board.
- Home milk delivery became a thing of the past as supermarket shopping became the major way of purchasing food.

A free-stall barn at Bohanan Farm, Contoocook, NH.

- The Fair Labor Standards Act was extended to include agriculture.
- Plastic milk containers were first introduced in 1964.
- New Hampshire Mastitis Committee was established in 1968 to monitor milk quality and educate farmers and was changed to the NH Dairy Practices Committee in 1975.

1970s

- High fuel prices and grain shortages set new input cost levels that never receded.
- No-tillage agriculture was popularized.

1980s

- The Milk Diversion Program of 1984 was implemented as an incentive for dairy farmers to reduce production.
- The National Dairy Promotion Program was introduced in 1984.
- The Dairy Termination Program of 1986 was put in place to reduce surplus milk supplies. New Hampshire farms submitted bids for ceasing production and 59 left the industry.
- There was a reduction and consolidation in the number of farmer cooperatives.

1990s

- There was increased pressure for dairy farms to remain competitive and profitable through the economy of scale.
- Rapid expansion of the dairy industry in California, New Mexico and Idaho made a major shift in centers of milk production.
- In 1994, USDA reorganized ASCS, SCS, and FmHA (Farmers Home Administration), resulting in FSA, NRCS and Rural Development.
- The bovine somatotropin (rBST) became commercially available to dairy producers as a way to augment milk production in 1994.
- The 1996 farm bill required the number of milk marketing orders be decreased to no more than 13 or 14 if California was included.
- The Northeast Dairy Compact was approved by each state legislature and Congress in 1996 and required that farmers receive a minimum price of 16.94 per cwt for class I milk. The money to support this floor price came from the market place. It expired in 2002 and was not reauthorized.

2000s

- The three Northeast Federal Milk Marketing Orders were combined into one and a component pricing system was adopted.
- The Milk Income Loss Contract (MILC) was implemented by the government to guarantee a minimum Class I price of milk for the first two million pounds shipped per farm.
- There was a movement toward a consolidation of the dairy processing industry to just a few national companies.
- New Hampshire changed from a semi-rural state to a suburban one.

- There were fewer choices for marketing milk and cyclical pricing became the norm.
- Emphasis on bio-security to control the spread of Johnes disease changed management practices on many farms.
- A growing demand for organic milk expanded throughout the country.
- UNH became the first Land Grant University to establish an organic dairy herd and shipped its first milk in January, 2007.
- In July of 2007, Governor John H. Lynch signed into law House Bill 407, which established the Emergency Dairy Assistance Program with an appropriation of $2.1 million. The program was in response to the extremely low farm milk prices in 2006, which resulted in severe financial stress for the state's dairy farms.

Jersey heifers at UNH organic dairy.

(Source: Granite State Dairymen Minutes, World Book Encyclopedia, USDA History of American Agriculture Timeline, 1607-2000)

The history of the New Hampshire fluid milk industry is revealed through the evolution of milk sales from doorstep delivery to distribution through gigantic shopping centers. This is best encapsulated in the detailed historical article, "From Dairy to Doorstep: The Processing and Sale of New Hampshire Dairy Products, 1860s to 1960s," written in 2003 by Judith N. Moyer for Historical New Hampshire, the journal of the New Hampshire Historical Society. She is an assistant research professor of history at the University of New Hampshire. The article is complete with old photos and worth reading.

(Courtesy NH Historical Society and Historic New England)

The NH Department of Agriculture Markets & Food is located in the State House Annex on 25 Capitol Street, Concord. This state agency monitors animal health, enforces regulations and promotes agriculture throughout the state.

State Government's Role in the Development of the New Hampshire Dairy Industry

Evolution of the Department of Agriculture

The New Hampshire Department of Agriculture, Markets & Food traces its origins to the mid-19th century, when the General Court established a Board of Agriculture composed of one farmer from each of the state's 10 counties. This board initially functioned primarily as an instrument of education, regularly conducting lectures and forums on agricultural subjects around the state, and publishing each year a volume containing the texts of many of the lectures.

In the 1890s the Board of Agriculture broadened its work to include efforts to rebuild the rural economy of the state, which had been devastated by national economic turmoil, heavy losses of men in the Civil War and continuing out-migration of population to urban areas and the West. The Board also began efforts to control diseases in livestock, crop pests and unscrupulous marketers of feeds and fertilizers.

The General Court in 1913 abolished the Board of Agriculture and created in its place a Department of Agriculture under the management of a commissioner of agriculture. The Department's first commissioner was Andrew L. Felker of Meredith, who in 40 years of service in the position, would write many laws to protect farmers and consumers and would develop a professional staff to administer the laws.

In 1919, the Department began publication of the Weekly Market Bulletin, a compendium of market news, farm commodities for sale and information for production agriculture. The Bulletin has been published every Wednesday since, and continues to serve as a primary vehicle for communication within the state's agricultural community.

Down through the 20th century there were many significant achievements for the department, but probably foremost would be eradication of major diseases of livestock and poultry through aggressive programs of surveillance and, where necessary, condemnation. New Hampshire was the first state to completely stamp out Brucellosis in cattle and led the nation in control of various other costly diseases.

Andrew L. Felker was the first NH Commissioner of Agriculture and served from 1913-1953. He established a lot of policy still in effect today.

Commissioner Felker was succeeded at the helm of the Department by Perley I. Fitts of Durham, 1953-1962; Frank T. Buckley of Derry 1962-1972; Howard C. Townsend of Lebanon, 1972-1982; and Stephen H. Taylor of Plainfield, 1982-2007. Lorraine Stuart Merrill became the first woman commissioner, sworn into office in December, 2007. (Text taken with permission in its entirety from the New Hampshire Department of Agriculture, Markets and Food web site: http://agriculture.nh.gov/)

Toward a Safe Milk Supply for New Hampshire

A Long, Hard Struggle for Better Bovine and Human Health

That New Hampshire consumers today enjoy supplies of safe, wholesome fresh milk and dairy products is a testament to a long and often bitterly fought struggle spanning much of the 20th century that involved farm leaders, veterinarians, physicians, public health officials, the food industry, Cooperative Extension and state and local politicians.

From a time when livestock disease was rampant and human health was at great risk from dangerous pathogens contained in farm milk and many processed dairy products, the public, now 100 years later, is able to depend upon a complex regulatory structure that assures them that the milk and dairy foods they consume are safe and high in quality and value.

Achieving today's level of food safety in the dairy sector is largely the result of visionary leadership afforded by a handful of New Hampshire citizens and public officials. They understood and appreciated the discoveries in the fields of bacteriology, chemistry, epidemiology and animal disease control and successfully applied this new knowledge to solving festering problems in the state's food supply.

Their efforts were often met with intense hostility, and initiatives drawing upon emerging scientific understanding often faced widespread political opposition, such that it took decades to achieve the beneficial results that today are taken for granted by the state's citizens.

Bringing New Hampshire a safe milk supply proceeded gradually along two fronts: controlling zoonotic diseases (diseases of animals which are transmissible to humans) in livestock, and making the milk safe as it moves from the animal to the consumer.

Two Terrible Diseases of Dairy Cattle

The campaign to improve the health of the nation's dairy herd and to control livestock disease transmissible to humans was largely centered on two diseases in the 20th century. Those diseases were tuberculosis and brucellosis.

In a 1923 message, U.S. Surgeon General James G. Townsend spoke of the nation's "milk problem" as being of such magnitude that it warranted engagement of "physicians, health officers, veterinarians, cattle owners, dairymen, the legal profession and every milk consumer." There is a milk problem, he said, "because 1. Milk is necessary; 2. Milk can be dangerous; 3. Milk spoils rapidly; and 4. Milk is consumed in the raw state."

By far the most serious single factor in the milk problem, Townsend said, was the relation it bears to the spread of tuberculosis, a disease characterized in the early 20th century as the "captain of the men of death" responsible for some 125,000 deaths yearly in this country. The disease was recognized as largely an ingestion infection, spread through food, drink and hand-to-mouth contact, and that it could be spread to humans through the milk of cows infected with the disease.

New Hampshire and most other states in the early 1900s had rudimentary mechanisms to inspect cattle for evidence of tuberculosis, but it was essentially through visual observation alone. New Hampshire's board of cattle commissioners could order a diseased animal destroyed, with the town government to compensate its owner, a provision which resulted in scant action ever being taken. The cattle commissioners could perform inspections of herds at the owner's request, a service that drew tepid interest as evidenced by the commissioner of agriculture's report for 1914 which showed only 313 herds inspected out of some 27,000 in the state.

The enactment of the federal meat inspection laws in 1906 provided the first effective means for ante- and post-mortem inspection of slaughter animals, and evidence of tuberculosis was cause for condemnation of a carcass. On-farm and custom slaughter and meat for intrastate commerce would remain largely outside of regulatory purview for most of the 20th century.

The field of veterinary medicine was just beginning to evolve from a lay vocation into a profession with credentialed practitioners by 1915, and this would begin to open the way for more scientific diagnoses of animal diseases. At the federal level restrictions were imposed on interstate movement of diseased animals, but within states the commerce in livestock was regulated in a haphazard way.

By the 1920s the concept of accreditation of dairy herds was taking hold, with farmers seeking verification by a veterinary professional of their herds being free of tuberculosis. But without a comprehensive testing program, it had to be assumed that tuberculosis lurked in every herd in the state. The NH Commissioner of Agriculture, Andrew L. Felker, in 1921 appointed Dr. Robinson Smith of Laconia to be state veterinarian, and Smith immediately set to work to eradicate tuberculosis in New Hampshire livestock. Smith established the entire state as a single eradication district, and launched a program of testing cattle on every farm in the state.

Cattle which tested positive for tuberculosis were condemned and the herds in which they resided were quarantined until retesting of all the animals showed them to be negative. Dr. Smith's aggressive strategy was met with considerable hostility in some quarters of the dairy industry, but by July 1933 New Hampshire became the 10th state to be awarded an Accredited Tuberculosis Area certificate. It took hundreds of thousands of tests on individual cows to weed out carriers of the disease, and to this day the state department of agriculture continues to test dairy herds to maintain New Hampshire accredited tuberculosis-free status.

On December 31, 1964, New Hampshire became the first state in the nation certified as "Accredited Bovine Tuberculosis-Free" by USDA. Dr. Clarence B. Dearborn, State Veterinarian, and Frank T. Buckley, Commissioner of Agriculture, are holding recognition plaques.

And it took a decision by the United States Supreme Court in a case originating in New Hampshire that affirmed the state veterinarian's power to enter any barn to inspect and test livestock suspected of harboring disease to end the resistance of some farmers to this vital public health function.

During the 1920s there were many dark days on New Hampshire dairy farms, as often testing revealed that 100 percent of the animals in a farmer's herd were infected with tuberculosis and would have to be appraised and slaughtered. Costs of indemnities were split between the state and federal governments.

Following his success with tuberculosis, Dr. Smith turned to brucellosis eradication, a challenge that would occupy him and his staff for nearly 30 years. Brucellosis when transmitted from cattle to humans becomes known as undulant fever, a serious affliction that can leave lifelong effects and result in death for some victims.

In the 1920s, brucellosis was called contagious infectious abortion, and later it was called Bang's Disease. Besides being a serious human health threat it was a devastating economic problem for farmers in terms of lost productivity. By 1928 some progressive New Hampshire dairy farmers were asking the state department of agriculture to give some form of official recognition to herd owners who on their own initiative cleaned up brucellosis on their farms.

In early 1929, the department under Felker and Smith adopted a plan for the eradication and control of bovine brucellosis, and soon a few farms submitted their herds to what became known as the agglutination test with the goal of establishing themselves as brucellosis-free. In the early 1930s uniform rules and procedures were adopted and many herds were voluntarily placed under state supervision and those meeting requirements were issued certificates attesting to their clean status.

No indemnities for condemned animals were paid for this voluntary certification and herd owners paid all the costs of the testing, which was supervised by the state department of agriculture.

In June 1934 the U.S. Congress passed what was known as the Jones-Connley Act, which provided for testing of herds for brucellosis and the removal by slaughter of condemned animals. All costs of performing tests were borne by the U.S. Department of Agriculture, and for all animals condemned the federal government paid a limit of $50 for a purebred and $25 for a grade animal.

But the brucellosis testing program remained a voluntary program, even though there was strong demand from dairy farmers for testing leading to certification of their herds as disease-free.

In 1937 Dr. Robert O. Blood, then a member of the state senate and later a governor, sought legislation that would have mandated that the state clean up brucellosis in a matter of three years. He was unsuccessful in that legislative session, but in 1939 a law was passed declaring that effective July 1, 1942, the entire state would become a quarantined area and that the state would proceed to test all cattle in the area. Reactors were to be sent to slaughter.

The World War II years saw the compulsory testing program take effect with a vengeance. Any herds where brucellosis reactors were found were condemned—inspectors would brand the letter "B" on the jowl of each animal and the cattle would be loaded and shipped off to slaughter.

Indemnity payments would help farmers re-establish herds, but rarely were they able to do so without severe financial stress. Some farmers lost three, four, even five herds as the testing program ruthlessly weeded out carriers of the disease.

In 1945 the legislature provided funding to pay for vaccination of all bovines four to eight months of age with what was called Strain 19 vaccine against brucellosis, and for permanent identification of all vaccinated animals. This vaccine gave considerable, but not total, immunity to recipient animals, and the state continued to support the program until the late 1980s.

On September 1, 1949, New Hampshire was declared a certified area, meaning the brucellosis contagion had been reduced to minuscule proportions, and in 1960 it became the first state in the Union to be officially recognized as a totally brucellosis-free state, with a State House ceremony involving Gov. Wesley Powell, agriculture commissioner Perley Fitts and dignitaries from USDA in Washington. In the period between 1934 and 1959 the state performed 2,862,805 individual agglutination tests and found 56,291 reactors.

State laboratories were used to test for cattle diseases. Left to right: Edward J. Daley, technician; John W. Monier, technician; Lawrence H. Blackmer, cattle appraiser; and Donald Thompson, bacteriologist.

Today brucellosis surveillance is performed through frequent testing of milk from individual farms. This testing work is carried out by the state Veterinary Diagnostic Laboratory at Durham.

Making Milk Safe for Everyone

As the 20th century dawned in New Hampshire and across the country, the highest concern among leaders in the field of public health was the safety of milk. As the population became ever more urban, it was moving further and further from the farms where milk was produced, causing it to be transported greater and greater distances at higher and higher temperatures.

Milk reaching urban consumers, particularly children, was increasingly contaminated, causing illness and death at alarming rates. Safety of the milk supply was a topic widely discussed and agonized over in the media, in the public health community and even in the courts, where a 1914 Illinois Supreme Court decision found "There is no article of food in more general use than milk; none whose impurity or unwholesomeness may more quickly, more widely, and more seriously affects the health of those who use it."

In New Hampshire in the first two decades of the 20th century milk for the non-farm population was provided through a few centralized distributing plants and several hundred individual farms which packaged and delivered milk door-to-door in nearby neighborhoods. Some New Hampshire farm milk was shipped by rail to large distributors in Boston and other milk was made into butter and cheese at small creameries scattered around the state.

There was virtually no regulation of these various distribution channels, and about the only means of protection for consumers was their own taste buds. By 1920, however, the idea of regulating the milk supply was taking hold across the country, concurrent with the refinement of methods for pasteurization of milk to control dangerous bacteria.

New Hampshire left regulation of milk up to cities and towns, and the result was that by 1930 the state was a patchwork of regulation and no regulation. Cities tended to develop regulation, first to cover larger centralized distribution facilities and then the dealers who peddled milk from their farms outside the city limits.

Smaller communities and rural areas saw no regulation during this early 20th century period despite growing evidence that unsanitary milk supplies posed significant risks to the consuming public. Abuses were widespread in the milk business in this time, with unscrupulous suppliers placing "Pasteurized" labels on unpasteurized milk and some adding chemicals such as formaldehyde to the milk to retard spoilage.

Refrigeration was rudimentary, with some farms relying on stored pond ice to chill milk, others spring water, still others nothing at all. Most retail containers were recycled, yet bottling facilities often lacked the means to adequately sanitize them.

Dairy services supervised by Dean G. Hammond included checking butterfat content as shown, as well as inspection of other dairy processing operations.

Early attempts at regulation of the milk supply were attacked as unconstitutional, unwarranted or un-American, and efforts in New Hampshire to impose even rudimentary rules were beaten back in several sessions of the legislature. But gradually public opinion and the wisdom of physicians and public health professionals began to hold sway, and by 1928 the State Board of Health could publish and distribute a booklet containing state sanitary food laws and regulations.

This volume laid down some basic provisions, including a requirement that milk be sold in sealed bottles, that cows and utensils be kept clean and that milk be cooled down to at least 50 degrees. A new set of regulations was posted in 1931, providing more specifics on procedures for pasteurization, and a ruling of the New Hampshire Supreme Court that year established once and for all that the state had the power to regulate the milk supply.

By 1934 the Board of Health was discovering that bacteria counts in milk samples were dropping sharply, although it also noted that some were still being found that indicated water was being added to the product. More than 55 pasteurization plants were closely monitored, and the majority of the milk reaching consumers was passing through these facilities.

Curiously, while regulation of the milk production, processing and distribution system in most states is the responsibility of the state department of agriculture, in New Hampshire this role is performed by the Department of Health and Human Services(HHS). While the agriculture agency was at the forefront in the battles against bovine diseases, it ceded the dairy sanitation function to an HHS ancestor agency in the 1930s and has had only a minor part in the work in the years since.

The Dairy Sanitation Program is part of the Bureau of Food Protection, located in the Department of Health & Human Services building on Hazen Drive in Concord. It has an important role in maintaining quality and a safe food supply.

In 1939 the U.S. Public Health Service published the Model Milk Health Ordinance—later to be called the Pasteurized Milk Ordinance—and began actively urging its adoption by the states. New Hampshire's response was led by Gilman Crowell, who held the title of state chemist and was an important cog in the state public health system. He convinced the legislature to join with other states in adopting this forward-looking measure to protect the consuming public.

There were still considerable volumes of raw milk being distributed by some farmers through the 1940s and 1950s in New Hampshire, although the number of these dealers was shrinking rapidly as consumers were indicating with their grocery purchases they wanted pasteurized product.

The watershed year for milk safety was 1973, when the U.S. Food and Drug Administration adopted a regulation that all milk moving in interstate commerce must be pasteurized. An objection from a "certified" raw milk producer won an exemption for this type of product until 1987, when the FDA, citing an extensive body of evidence linking certified raw milk with human disease and under pressure from a federal court, issued a final rule banning interstate commerce in raw milk.

Today no raw milk can legally be sold across state lines for consumer use, but a number of states, including New Hampshire, allow limited intrastate sale of raw milk. New Hampshire permits on-farm sale direct to consumers so long as the purchaser is informed of the risks.

Regulation of milk and dairy products has proved to be one of the great public health achievements of the 20th century. Data show that in 1938, 25 percent of all disease outbreaks from contaminated food and water were attributable to milk; by 2002 that number was down to about one percent, abundant proof that the regulatory system established across the country has worked effectively in the broad public interest.

(Department of Agriculture Reports 1879-1968; State of New Hampshire, Reports of State Board of Health, 1924-1939; Weisbecker, A., 2007, April).

Continuing Leadership in Animal Health

The two big cattle diseases that affect human health—tuberculosis and brucellosis, have been eradicated and successfully kept out of New Hampshire herds for many years. But increased global travel and trade in animals and food products demand diligence and surveillance to prevent introduction or transmission of new disease threats. Changes in diseases and farming practices have also led to new or increased spread of other bovine diseases, such as Johne's (Mycobacterium paratuberculosis) and BVD (bovine virus diarrhea). These diseases can have serious economic and animal health impacts on a herd. Research has been inconclusive on whether Johne's may have a connection to human health as well.

New Hampshire has been a leader in Johne's testing and control during Steve Taylor's tenure as commissioner. State Veterinarian Cliff McGinnis initiated and implemented the state's voluntary program with federal funding, in collaboration with the New Hampshire Veterinary Diagnostic Laboratory at the University of New Hampshire.

His successor, Dr. Stephen Crawford, continued the focused and collaborative approach established by Dr. McGinnis of helping producers with testing and veterinary consulting services to interpret results and make management improvements in their herds. This aggressive approach to implementing the national voluntary Johne's control program was well received by the state's progressive dairy industry, resulting in New Hampshire having the highest level of participation of all states in the voluntary federal Johne's program.

Given this success, State Veterinarian Stephen Crawford has set a goal for New Hampshire to become a pilot state for Johne's control. "New Hampshire was first to eradicate TB," Crawford was quoted in *Hoard's Dairyman*. "The dairy industry here is doing a great job of management and can provide a model." As of 2006 nearly 60% of the state's 130 herds were enrolled, plus another 14 had participated and then lapsed. Achieving significant further gains in controlling and eradicating Johne's disease will depend on the level of continuing federal funding.

Commissioner Stephen H. Taylor

Serving as commissioner for 25 years, Plainfield native Stephen H. Taylor became an icon of New Hampshire and its agriculture. First appointed in 1982 by Gov. Hugh Gallen, Taylor was reappointed to four additional successive five-year terms by governors from both parties, until announcing his retirement in 2007. The length of his tenure is second only to New Hampshire's first commissioner of agriculture, Andrew Felker.

A long-time farmer, newspaperman, and public official, Taylor was known as an articulate spokesman and leader of agriculture in the state. A graduate of the University of New Hampshire, he was an advocate for the vital importance of public education and higher education, research, and extension to agriculture and the people of the state. Under his leadership, the department became the Department of Agriculture, Markets & Food.

The department's staff has implemented significant programs in promoting the health of the animal and plant industries; expanding markets and interest in locally produced New Hampshire foods and other farm products; regulating pesticide use, market weights and measures, farm input products such as feed and fertilizers; solving conflicts and promoting conservation of soil, water, and agricultural lands; and forging connections and communication with other state and federal agencies, agricultural and other interest groups around the state.

Stephen H. Taylor, Commissioner, 1982-2007.

He and his wife Gretchen, with their sons and their families, operate a dairy and maple farm in the Meriden Village area of Plainfield.

Feeding molasses on forages to dairy cows in a stanchion barn in the late 1940s or early 1950s.

The New Hampshire Dairy Industry

The New Hampshire dairy industry is located primarily in the Connecticut River Valley on the state's western borders and along the Merrimack River Valley in the center of the state. Other farms are scattered in areas of open, fertile land (see figure 1). Dairy farming is an "extensive form" of agriculture that requires many acres for crop production. The average dairy farm in New Hampshire uses about two acres of tillage to support the forage needs of each dairy cow and her replacement. Some farms use a rotational pasture system for summer feeding and allow about one acre per cow for grazing, with the other acre used to produce the feed that is stored for the winter.

Production Practices

Unlike farms in the Midwest, most New Hampshire dairy farms don't produce their own concentrate (grain feed) and have the added expense of buying this essential part of a cow's diet. Concentrate is fed in addition to forage to meet the nutrient needs of a cow for maximum production. Forages include corn silage and hay crops. Corn silage is generally

Tie-stall housing, Stonewall Farm, Keene, NH.

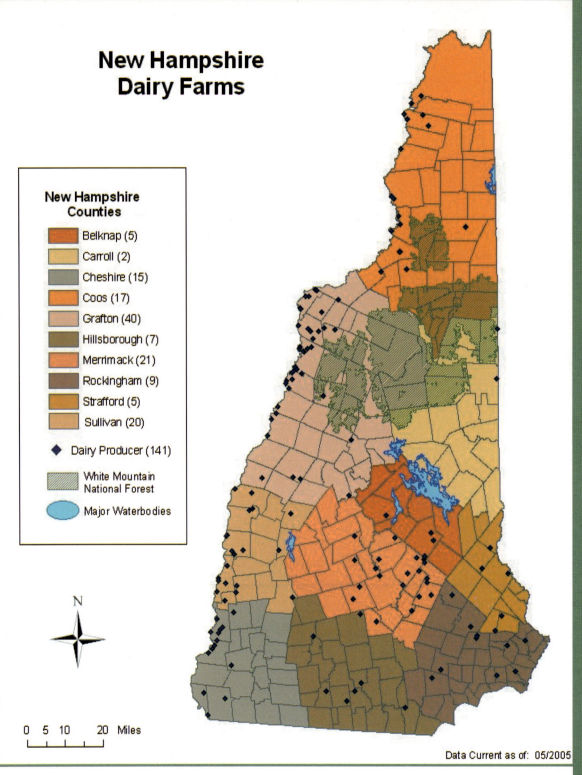

Figure 1. Distribution of Dairy Farms throughout New Hampshire. Locations verified using Global Positioning Systems (GPS). Information provided by NH Department of Agriculture, Markets & Food.

a large part of most rations because corn yields 6 - 8 tons of dry matter feed per acre, equal to about 21 tons of silage as harvested. Hay crops yield about 1.8 tons of dry matter per acre or around 2 tons per acre of dry hay (NASS N.E. Bul., 2004, p.39). Much of the hay crop for dairy animals is harvested as haylage, where the grass is chopped in a wilted stage and put in a silo to ferment. Hay is dried naturally in the field and depends on favorable weather conditions to produce good quality.

Free-stall barn at the Tullar Farm in Orford, NH.

The average dairy farm in New Hampshire consists of about 115 head of milking animals and nearly that number of heifers to replace older cows, culled for health, breeding or production reasons. The herd sizes range from 12-15 cows to the largest of 1,000 cows, which is located in Coos County. The majority of the cows are housed in a free-stall barn system, in which the animals are free to roam in and out of their stalls and access feed at a feed bunk as they choose. This type of housing lends itself to mechanization, and the cows are milked in a "parlor" where the person milking the cows stands in a pit and is able to attach the milking machine without bending. There are still some farms that use tie-stalls, where the cow is served its ration and milked in the same place. In both situations, the farm are inspected by the NH Department of Public Health and must meet strict sanitary requirements for producing milk. Great measures are also taken to address cow comfort, as farmers care about their animals, and well-managed animals are more productive.

A double-10, quick-release, herringbone milking parlor with a walk-in vestibule entrance at the Tullar Farm in Orford, NH.

Business Arrangements

On the average, farms have about 44 milking cows per worker, so the average farm consists of the operator and two employees (Northeast Dairy Farm Summary, 2006, p. 37). According to the U.S. Agricultural Census (2002, p.147), dairy farms in New Hampshire employ 1,266 full and part-time workers. In addition, the dairy industry requires many other support people and supply industries for feed, fertilizer, veterinary services, supplies and building materials. Most of these dairy farms are family operations. In New Hampshire the ownership arrangements are: sole proprietorships, 68 percent; partnerships, 21 percent; famly corporations, 5.5 percent; trusts and estates, 5 percent; and nonfamily held corporations, .5 percent (U.S. Agricultural Census, 2002, pp. 145-147).

A tie-stall barn at Jolyon Johnson Farm, Sunapee, NH.

Dairy producer field meeting circa 1940s to mid 1950s.

Producer - Distributors

Most New Hampshire milk is marketed either through farmer cooperatives or independent processors. Twelve dairy farms, however, are classified as producer-distributors; they produce their own milk and market it directly as bottled milk or as milk products they process. Several others are looking at value-added opportunities. The Westover and Graves families of Great Brook Dairy in Walpole are planning to open a dairy store on the farm and sell raw milk. Doug and Deb Erb of Springvale Farm in Landaff are getting facilities ready to make farmstead cheese. Most of these farms also rely on cooperatives or independent handlers to purchase their excess milk or supply additional milk to meet their marketing needs. These are illustrated below.

McNamara Dairy, Plainfield, NH - McNamara Dairy processes about 90 percent of the milk produced by its 120-head of Holstein cows. Patrick McNamara, top left, is shown putting up quart and two quart and glass bottles of whole milk. They also produce low fat, skim, chocolate milk and eggnog in season. They market throughout the Upper Valley of New Hampshire and retail at their farm store.

(Photo courtesy of Marcus Lovell-Smith)

Boggy Meadow Farm, Walpole, NH - Boggy Meadow Farm cheese is produced at the farm in Walpole, NH. Over 200 head of Holstein cattle are milked at the farm with approximately 10 percent of the milk used in the production of aged, raw-milk Swiss cheese. The cheese is marketed through specialty cheese shops, select supermarkets and sold retail on the honor system at the farm store.

Sandwich Creamery, North Sandwich, NH - Tom and Lisa Merriman, shown top right, operate Sandwich Creamery. They sometimes use the milk from their small herd of four cows or purchase milk from a dairy cooperative. It is a small and efficient operation that makes aged cheddar cheese, smoked cheddar, Caerphilly, Brie, Coulommier, and several soft spread cheeses, as well as several flavors of ice cream. The Sandwich Creamery ships cheese orders nationwide and markets their cheeses at their honor-system farm store, supermarkets and farmers' markets. Ice cream shops in the area feature its ice cream.

Hatchland Farm, Haverhill, NH - The farm has a herd of 325 Holstein milking cows and raises the majority of the feed they use on approximately 800 acres, owned and rented in the precinct of Haverhill. The dairy uses all the milk produced on the home farm to process whole milk, low fat milk, skim and chocolate milk. The processing plant has a total of 14,250 square feet, and has vat pasteurizers, bottlers, and a walk-in cooler. The milk is bottled in pints, one and two quarts, and gallons in plastic and glass bottles. It is distributed in New Hampshire as well as the Boston area.

Connolly Brothers, Temple, NH - The Connollys, shown left to right in the top right photo, Patrick, Michael and Chris, have a lot of neighbors who enjoy visiting the only dairy farm in Temple. People were so interested in supporting the farm that the Connolly brothers decided to make some value-added products. They built a processing room at the end of the cow barn, which had previously been a sawdust shed and storage area. Their processing room was certified in March of 2004 and they started selling ice cream that summer. They also sell raw skim and whole milk and separated cream.

They milk 45 head of Jerseys and sell about 50 percent of their milk production as value-added products. The rest of their milk goes through the Dairy Farmers of America (DFA) Cooperative to the HP Hood plant in Concord. The ice cream and milk is sold primarily at the farm store on the honor system, with some ice cream going to ice cream shops and other stores. They offer 25 different flavors of ice cream, ice cream bars, ice cream sandwiches and pre-frozen sundaes.

(Mark Jenson photo courtesy of Echo Farm)

Echo Farm, Hinsdale, NH – This farm has often been called a "4-H project gone wild." It began with a 4-H herd and the Hodge and Schofield families working together to start the dairy herd and milk processing. About 20 percent of the milk from the Jersey, Milking Shorthorn, and Guernsey herd is made into several flavors of pudding and sold as Echo Farm Pudding throughout the Northeast and selected regions across the U.S. Shown in the top right photo, left to right, are Courtney Hodge, Gordon Schofield, Shelley Schofield, Beth Hodge and Joshua Martin.

The Temple-Wilton Community Farm, Wilton, NH - The farm is managed by Lincoln Geiger along with Dan Zabara and Anthony Graham. This is a Community Supported Agriculture (CSA) facility with 105 member families. The farm started in 1986, supplying a small number of families with milk and vegetables in exchange for an annual fee. It has grown over the years, becoming a licensed producer-distributor in 2005 that allows the farm to make yogurt with surplus milk that is pasteurized. It is a self-sustaining operation, milking 14 head of dairy cattle of various breeds. Shown in the top right photo, left to right, are Lincoln Geiger and Dan Zabara.

Flying Cloud Dairy, LLC, Alstead, NH – Flying Cloud Dairy began in 2000 and is a joint venture of Bill Jahos, shown in the top left photo, member/manager and Dave French, member/investor. It is a hillside farm using rotational grazing and has a milking herd of about 20 Jerseys. Flying Cloud Dairy is one of the early organic dairies in the state. As a licensed producer-distributor, it fills glass and plastic bottles directly from the tank, selling raw milk weekly to customers who come to the farm. The other production is sold to Organic Valley/CROPP Cooperative.

The Sherman Farm, East Conway, NH – The farm reduced the size of its dairy herd over the years and expanded into vegetables and added value to its milk production. Al and Phyllis Sherman, shown in the top right photo, along with their daughter Kathy, grow vegetables and operate the farm store. In 1997 they started a milk bottling arrangement with Smiling Hill Farm in North Scarborough, Maine and market over 50 percent of the milk produced by the dairy tenant this way. The milk is hauled to Maine by a Sherman Farm employee who works at the bottling plant. He returns with the processed product. They make whole, skim, reduced-fat, banana, strawberry, chocolate, low-fat chocolate, vanilla, coffee, blueberry and orange milk, as well as half-and-half, and eggnog in season. The milk is marketed at the farm store and distributed through 12-14 stores in the region. One distributor sells the milk through a home delivery service and to stores, and farmers' markets in Southern New Hampshire.

(Photo courtesy of Stonewall Farm)

Stonewall Farm, Keene, NH – The farm first started in 1989 and then set-up as a nonprofit education center. Its mission is to keep people connected to the land and aware of the role local agriculture plays in their lives. Staff educators share the importance of dairy farming with up to 8,000 school children per year. Stonewall Farm grows certified, naturally-grown vegetables offered through a Community Supported Agriculture (CSA) farm stand and farmers' market. A new dairy complex was built in 2000 and houses a herd of 30 Holstein cattle, which are certified organic. Stonewall Farm is a licensed producer-distributor selling over 25 gallons of raw milk per day. The raw milk is bottled directly from the bulk tank into glass bottles, using a special filler valve. The milk is stored in a cooler and sold at the farm store. The remaining milk production on the farm is shipped to Organic Valley Cooperative. Shown in the top right photo is Wendy French, herdsperson.

Walpole Creamery, LLC, Walpole, NH - Tom and Sharlene Beaudry, of Echo Moon Farm, along with friends Steve Caswell and David Westover, started producing ice cream in September, 2006. The creamery is located in an industrial building on Route 12 in Walpole. The ice cream plant was a way to make a value-added product from the milk produced at Echo Moon Farm from their 40-head Holstein cattle. Currently, 5 percent of the milk production is used to make ice cream. They pasteurize the milk and make their own mixes for 18 flavors. The ice cream is sold at the ice cream shop at the plant and to over 80 stores in the area. Shown, top right, are Steve Caswell and Tom Beaudry making ice cream.

Robie Farm, Piermont, NH - Members of the Robie family have been farming along the scenic Connecticut River since 1861. The current owners are the fifth generation and work with their sons, the sixth generation. In an attempt to capture more value-added income for their milk in times of low milk prices, they became a certified cheese-maker in March 2007. They added 15 Jersey cows, fed non-fermented feeds to provide the high solids milk used in the cheese enterprise. The youngest son, Mark, shown above, has been studying artisan cheese production. He uses a cheese-making room constructed at the barn. Mark specializes in Toma, an aged raw-milk Italian cheese, as well as a traditional English cheese known as Swaledale.

The oldest son, Freeman, makes ice cream at the farm using locally grown fruit and other creative combinations. The lower level of the old horse barn, attached to the family home, has been converted to a farm store for selling cheese, raw milk, baked goods, beef, pork, sausage, ice cream and vegetables, all of which are made or grown on the Robie Farm.

In the early 1900s, dairy producers switched from making butter on the farm to bottling milk. Each farm had its own embossed (image stamped into the glass) or ink logo with the farm name. Some bottles had a cream-top, a swelled-neck section with a restricted base that collected cream that could be dipped out with a special short ladle. Richard Clark of Bedford, NH has documented over 918 different types of milk bottles used in New Hampshire. Shown above are bottles at the Swain Farm, Sanbornton, NH. This farm is also building a processing room and getting ready to market milk from the farm.

Filling an upright silo with grass silage using a cutter-blower in the 1940s or early 1950s.

Commercial Processors

There are five major commercial milk processors in New Hampshire inspected by the NH Dairy Sanitation Program. These companies may or may not purchase milk from New Hampshire farms, but they are an important part of the state's dairy economy. They produce milk products on a commercial basis distributed around the state, region or nation. These include:

HP Hood LLC, Concord, NH - This plant has been an important player in milk processing since its beginning as the Concord Dairy, and then under its many years of operation by the Weeks family and then Crowley Foods. It is now the largest processor of New Hampshire milk in the state. It currently processes more than 600,000 pounds of milk a day, sourced from local New Hampshire and New England farms.

Bishop's Homemade Ice Cream, Littleton, NH - Bishop's Ice Cream is one of the few companies in New Hampshire that makes its own ice cream. In operation since 1976, it produces ice cream seasonally in its plant behind its ice cream store on 183 Cottage Street in Littleton. It purchases an ice cream base from HP Hood in Concord and Oakhurst Dairy and makes 72 flavors on a rotating basis. It sells ice cream from its shop in Littleton and distributes to New Hampshire and Vermont vendors. It is a well known name in ice cream in the North Country.

(Photo courtesy of Stonyfield Farm Yogurt)

Stonyfield Farm, Londonderry, NH - 2008 marks Stonyfield's 25th year, with an international reputation as the world's leading organic yogurt manufacturer. Its 100 percent organic line includes organic yogurt, drinkable smoothies, YoBaby and YoKids brands, frozen yogurt, ice cream, cultured soy and milk. The company follows environmentally-sound practices and recently installed the fifth-largest solar array in New England to help power its production plant. Its organic milk comes from Organic Valley/CROPP, a farmer-owned cooperative, and it has actively worked to increase organic milk production in New Hampshire.

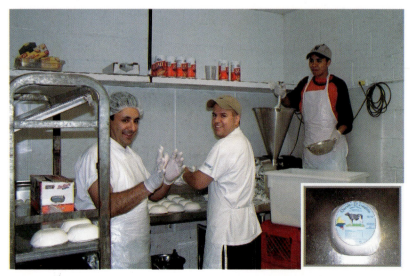

Quesito El Establo, Salem, NH – Tomas Arango started making Spanish cheese in 2002 in one section of the Turner Dairy plant and purchased milk from the owner. Now that the Turner Dairy facility is only a milk shipping warehouse, Tomas purchases pasteurized Oakhurst milk in gallon plastic bottles from the distributor located on site. The cheese is a natural Spanish cheese made at a low temperature with only cheese cultures and salt. It is sliced and put on bread or salads. He produces about 250 pounds a day, two days a week, with two helpers. The cheese is delivered to small stores in Massachusetts. Left to right are Tomas Arango, Wilberto Medina and Fredy Taborda.

(Photo courtesy of Blake's Creamery)

Blake's Creamery, Manchester, NH – Edward C. Blake founded Blake's Creamery in 1900, making it one of New Hampshire's oldest milk and cream plants. The plant and administrative offices are located at the original site at 46 Milford Street with a restaurant in front on 353 South Main Street in Manchester. In the early years, the creamery bought milk from farmers in North Haverhill, NH. Now it purchases milk and ice cream mix from HP Hood. Blake's manufactures more than 80 flavors of ice cream and other frozen products. In 1963 the company introduced its super-premium line of ice cream and has several exclusive, trademarked formulas. In addition to the restaurant located at the headquarters, they have two others in Manchester, NH.

Granite State Dairy Promotion is funded by New Hampshire dairy producers to promote the consumption of milk and dairy products. In 2007, they revamped the dairy trailer to give a fresh image for promoting the dairy industry.

Old processing plant design for pasteurizing milk.

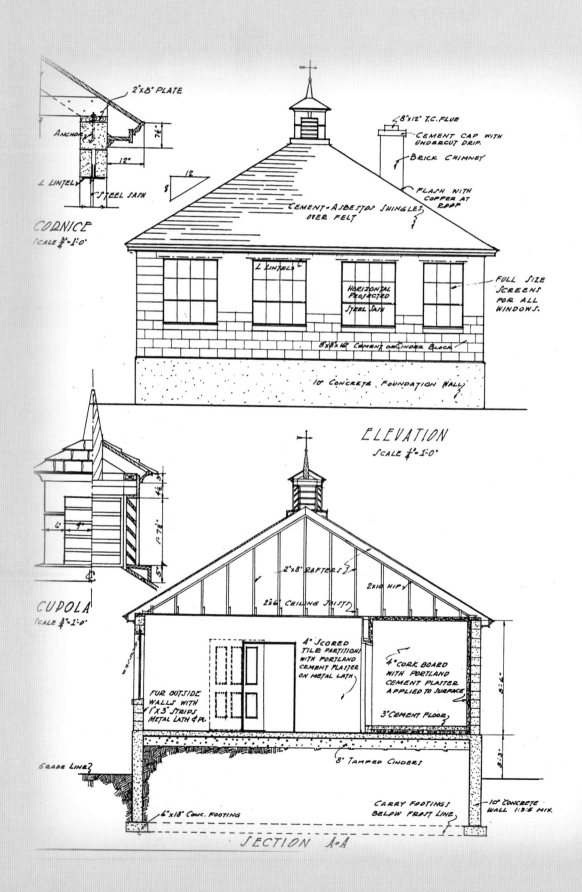

Bulk milk tanker truck picking up milk at the Crete Farm in Boscawen, NH.

Milk Marketing

Milk's appearance as simply a homogenous commodity can be deceiving. It is a highly-perishable, bulky product produced every day in varying amounts on a large number of independent farms before being processed by a limited number of dealers, making the story of milk pricing one of intrigue and drama.

Early farms in New England were self-sufficient, with farm families producing all their food and clothing needs. Bartering occurred at the country store where they would exchange butter, pork and beef for salt, sugar and liquors.

Between 1810 and 1860, the Industrial Revolution changed the country. Connecticut, Massachusetts and Rhode Island's populations rose by an additional one million. Some farms were large enough to subdivide, allowing one or two sons to remain on the farm. At the same time, many sons and daughters left the farm to join immigrants in emerging cities working in the textile industry, or as clerks and teachers. By 1850, two-thirds of the women had left their hometowns and married men who weren't connected to the farm (Dublin, 1996).

As the population increased in metropolitan areas, the cows grazing on both Boston and New York City public commons disappeared, and the dreadful 'swill milk'[1] was gradually replaced with what was advertised at the time as milk produced on "pure feed and pasture"(Selitzer, 1976, p. 37).

Farmers located some distance from growing communities processed their own milk or sent it to processing plants to make butter and cheese. Those located closer to the cities would haul their milk by horse and wagon to the population centers, where they would use a dipper to sell directly from cans to customers. The farmers soon found they were unable to keep up with the demands of the exploding populations.

Introduction of Railroads

Sensing an opportunity to increase their business, in April of 1838, the owners of the Boston to Worcester (Massachusetts) railroad started hauling milk as regular baggage, bringing new opportunities in milk marketing. Initially much of the milk soured on the trip because no cooling was provided during the summer, except for some limited icing. In the winter, blankets and lanterns were used to try to keep the milk from freezing. Railroads rapidly opened new markets. Farmers who had previously processed small quantities of milk into cheese and butter at home or small processing plants were able to send their milk into a more lucrative "fluid" or beverage market.

By 1850, it was estimated the great majority of farms were located within 10 to 12 miles of a railroad track. While this allowed farmers to take advantage of more distant markets, it also brought competition, allowing products from outside the region to compete with local production. The sheep that grazed on the hillsides were gradually replaced with cows when trains brought less expensive wool produced in Ohio to the New England textile mills.

Marketing Milk Entrepreneurs

It was about this time that young Harvey P. Hood left his family homestead in Vermont and became a driver for a bakery route in Boston. After two years, he had saved enough money to start a milk route and founded Hood Milk Company in 1846. Upset about the quantity and quality of milk available, he purchased a dairy farm in Derry, NH, and gradually starting acquiring milk from neighboring farms.

In 1860, Hood arranged to have a special milk car built that held 8,000 quarts of milk. Every morning he would collect milk, load the cans into the freight car and attach it to the one train a day that left Derry for Boston. He sat at a desk in the freight car working on his accounts as the train made its trip. Finely chopped ice would cool the milk in summer and a wood burning stove provided heat in the winter, giving residents their first constant supply of quality milk (Selitzer, 1976, p. 113).

This dedication to quality was appreciated by a city that in 1859 appointed the first milk inspector in the United States. David Whiting, a farmer from Wilton, NH, soon followed Hood in the "milk contracting" business. By 1898, there were seven organizations, including three controlled by Whiting, which handled 75 percent of the milk sold to 597 peddlers in Boston (Barnhart, 1947, p. 15).

Shipping milk in cans was both cumbersome and costly. Milk had to be transferred from the railroad to the plant, which required strong men and wagons. The cans cost $6 a piece with only a maximum lifespan of four years (Selitzer, 1976, p.193). Distributing milk was also labor intensive. For example, in Boston in 1886, approximately 3,350 people were employed in distributing 180,565 quarts of milk daily (Selitzer, 1976, p. 17). Still it wasn't until 1903 that tank car shipments of milk occurred and finally in 1910, the Whiting Milk Company introduced the first commercially-built tank car specially designed to carry milk (Selitzer, 1976, p.193). By charging less for hauling milk in refrigerated cars than in cans, the reduced risk of contamination and better temperature control, rail transportation gained favor with health officials and the public.

Along railroad tracks, more sophisticated receiving stations gradually replaced the small can platforms. An article reprinted from the Albany Cultivator by the New England Farmer on Sept. 6, 1943 states:

> *Prior to 1870 all of the milk consumed in Boston came from a distance of not more than 65 miles. By 1890 the Boston and Maine railroad was bringing milk from a distance of 150 miles and in 1910 of 275 miles. In 1916, 90 percent of the milk received in Boston and 98 percent of New York City's milk supply arrived by train.*

Even though the milk truck first emerged in the 1930s, trains continued to haul milk for several more decades until the widespread adoption of the refrigerated bulk tank[2] replaced the milk can in the 1950s.

Rise of Milk Cooperatives

Milk consumption is inelastic, with demand staying fairly constant regardless of price. When cows were let out to green pastures in the spring, they would produce as much as 40 percent more milk than they did in the winter, creating a "spring flush" or oversupply of milk. Problems in marketing milk occurred about as soon as the milk dealers started buying it.

While all milk was basically the same, the price that two farmers received for their milk varied depending on how the milk was used. Dealers supplying milk for the higher quality drinking or fluid market, paid higher prices and accepted enough farmers to meet their needs during periods of milk shortages. By doing this, when the flush occurred dealers had too much milk. This caused them to either manufacture milk into lower valued products or sometimes refuse milk or not return milk cans to farmers, forcing them to feed their milk to animals. Dealers who regularly manufactured milk products, which had a longer shelf life, paid farmers less for their milk because of consumer resistance to paying higher prices.

Many New England farmers recognized that unless they were able to join together, these unacceptable practices would continue. In 1867, one of the earliest cooperative type organizations in the country, the Milk Producers' Association of Massachusetts and New Hampshire, was organized based on a European model. It served as an agent to distribute milk to various milkmen (Barnhart, 1947, p. 15).

By the 1880s, a successor organization, the New England Milk Producers Union, which merged with the Boston Cooperative Milk Producers in 1899, negotiated a contract with dealers that paid farmers more money for the milk primarily used for drinking or fluid purposes than milk used for butter.

They also negotiated an operating reserve and allowed for deductions for handling charges and transportation costs that varied by the distance milk was shipped.

In 1901, the program ended because dealers had expanded the milk shed (the area supplying milk to the city) and an estimated 25 percent of the milk on the market was surplus (Barnhart, 1947, pp. 15 - 20). From 1905 until 1910, the Boston market experimented with the Knapp Plan that contracted with farmers for a specific amount of milk. The market then returned to the simple flat pricing method of paying an equal price for all milk for two years, before the market became organized in 1916 (Barnhart, 1947, p. 21).

Some farmers, originally accused of violating the Sherman Anti-trust Act of 1890, reorganized as the New England Milk Producers' Association (NEMPA). They had been part of the original Union dissolved in 1912. In October of 1916, they held a successful milk strike resulting in the formation of a joint committee of farmers and handlers to calculate a price paid to farmers. With the success of this program under its belt, in August 1917, NEMPA and the milk dealers agreed to a pricing plan that for the first time established a single pricing point in Boston, instituted hauling charges, cooperative dues and a can service charge.

To assure it could control any surplus milk, it also invested in manufacturing plants to deal with the surplus milk. In the May, 1917, issue of the *Dairyman,* NEMPA claimed "a membership of nearly 10,000 farmers living in a territory from Aroostook County, Maine to southwestern Connecticut; and from Boston to Burlington and Newport, Vermont; and Cambridge, New York on the west," (Barnhart, 1947, pp. 20-23).

The successful milk strike spurred new enthusiasm for cooperatives. In 1919, two other well-known New England milk cooperatives, St. Albans Cooperative and Cabot Creamery, were established. These cooperatives worked on the principle that they were simply an extension of the members' farms. Their farmer members invested in the operations and shared in the profits or losses from the cooperative's activities. Cabot Creamery did this by requiring its original 94 Vermont farmers to invest $3,700 on the basis of $5 per cow, plus one cord of wood each to fire the boiler, to establish their first building (Duffey, 2000).

Congress Steps Into Milk Marketing

In 1917, the United States was at war and feeding people was an important priority for the country. A newly-appointed Federal Food Administrator made it clear he preferred dealing with cooperatives rather than individual farmers. The milk dealers were challenging the ability of the cooperative associations to organize, charging they were in violation of the Sherman Anti-trust Act of 1890, because they were attempting to increase and fix the price of milk. The cooperatives fired back that the Clayton Act of 1914 permitted non-stock cooperatives to bargain collectively for prices on behalf of their members.

To settle the conflict after years of debate and rewrites, U. S. Senator Arthur Capper from Kansas, and Congressman Andrew Volstead from Minnesota, successfully enacted the Capper-Volstead Act on February 18, 1922. Hailed as the "Magna Carta" of cooperatives, this legislation explicitly authorized and sanctioned the elimination of competition among farmers who work together through cooperative associations.

The legislation appeared to work before the Great Depression, when several milk cooperatives joined together, formally adopting a classified pricing plan. This paid farmers more money for Grade A fluid milk than milk used for manufactured products, pooled receipts so farmers received similar prices and required dealers to share information on their use and sales. While the program is credited with preventing dairy farmers from experiencing the economic distress that grain, cotton and tobacco farmers suffered during the 1920s, farmers never had confidence in the program because dealers refused to open their books to audit and there were no enforcement procedures. In addition, some independent farmers supplied milk directly to dealers, allowing them to undercut the cooperative prices.

The Great Depression

During the Great Depression, the classified pricing systems broke down as the demand for milk drastically dropped and desperate farmers took any price offered just to have some income. Average milk prices dropped 31 percent between 1929 and 1933, putting farmers and rural communities in economic distress (Manchester, 1983). Cooperatives turned to Congress for help. Even though agriculture no longer employed over half the work force in the United States as it had in the 19th century, it was still by far the biggest employer geographically, and one of the most important elements in the nation's gross national product (Futurecasts, 2001).

The first piece of legislation in President Franklin Roosevelt's New Deal was the Agricultural Adjustment Act of 1933 (AAA), which formally brought the government into milk marketing. It had a provision authorizing the Secretary of Agriculture to enter into voluntary marketing agreements and licensing that required milk dealers in designated areas to pay farmers a "classified price" for milk.

Because the classified or blend price is determined by multiplying the price paid by the total volume of milk used for beverages or in processing in a market area, it reduced the pressure on farmers to sell their milk only for higher-priced fluid milk. It also recognized the investment farmers made to meet the higher sanitary standards required to produce beverage quality or Grade A milk and in the facilities to process the milk. While the proposal appeared to address the concerns of everyone, in reality the marketing agreements were only adopted in a few milksheds.

The AAA provision, which historians believe had a great influence on milk pricing, was the idea of tying the price of milk to "parity." In dollar-and-cents terms, this is the ratio between what farmers receive for their milk and the prices of things they buy based on the pre-war years of 1910-1914. Until the 1980s, parity was used to set support prices and loan rates.

Fearing the Supreme Court would declare the Agricultural Adjustment Act unconstitutional, in 1935 Congress amended it allowing for voting by producers, fixing of minimum prices, bloc voting, payments to cooperatives, and seasonal and geographical provisions for price differentials. They replaced licenses with "Orders" issued by the Secretary of Agriculture that required all dealers to participate in market-wide pooling. This key provision, which remains in the Order language today, places all milk dealers in the same competitive position because they were all required to pay the same minimum price for milk. This allowed them to focus on marketing instead of worrying about another dealer being able to undercut them on price.

Because of the Order provision, farmers continued to receive a blend price for all the milk they produced, and milk prices were based on how far the purchasing plant was from areas with a concentration of consumers (e.g. Boston). Another provision of the 1935 Act allowed the federal government to purchase excess dairy products and distribute them to relief efforts.

After the Supreme Court ruled that the 1933 Act was unconstitutional because of its overly broad delegation of authority from Congress to the Executive Branch, Congress adopted the Agriculture Marketing Agreement Act of 1937 (AMAA), with the focus of creating orderly markets. It reaffirmed the marketing agreement provisions of the 1933 Act and redefined the process for establishing Federal Milk Marketing Orders with three major objectives:

1) To assure consumers of an adequate supply of wholesome milk at a reasonable price.

2) To promote greater producer price stability and orderly marketing.

3) To provide adequate producer prices to ensure adequate current and future Grade A milk supplies.

These objectives are achieved through:

- *Classified pricing:* Minimum pay prices established for milk and milk components according to what dairy products they are used to produce.

- *Pooling:* Within each order, producers receive a uniform price for their milk (of equal quality and composition) or milk components regardless of how their milk is used.

The program worked. In 1947, an estimated 13,009 producers pooled in Boston 1,331,423,000 pounds of milk that was sold to the consumer for an average of 19½ cents per quart (Roadhouse and Henderson, 1950, p. 550).

Federal Milk Marketing Orders are unique in several ways. While Congress makes broad policy recommendations, the Act authorizes the Secretary of Agriculture "to establish and maintain such orderly marketing conditions …as will provide, in the interests of producers and consumers, an orderly flow of the supply …to avoid unreasonable fluctuations in supplies and prices" (United States Code, 2006). To accomplish this, the Secretary is charged with using a hearing process to create the Order regulations that can only be implemented with the approval by referendum of two-thirds of the farmers in the Order. Another unique feature of Orders is that no federal funds are used to administer its provisions. Instead, milk dealers pay the cost of administrating the program because it creates a level pricing playfield for them.

It was around this time that states adopted their own pricing regulations in an effort to further support farmers, but most have been eliminated. Maine, California and Pennsylvania continue to operate programs in conjunction with the Federal Order program. California maintains an independent pricing program. Other states and some cities have laws regulating the retail price of milk. In addition, health departments nationwide enacted and enforced milk control ordinances, guaranteeing that milk is a safe and wholesome product.

World War II

The Second World War brought new demands to the industry. With higher incomes due to wartime employment, demand for dairy products grew domestically, and the military was eating all the dairy products they could find. Ice cream made from dried whole milk was a particular favorite, with the Navy spending one million dollars to build an ice cream parlor as a morale booster. The United States was also exporting cheese, butter, canned milk and dried milk. In 1943, five percent of the nation's butter was sent to Russia where it was used to feed the Red Army (Seltizer, 1976, pp. 335-337).

With competition from manufactured products for fluid milk, Federal Orders set fluid or bottling milk prices at a fixed amount above manufacturing grade. Parity was set at 85 percent with government incentive payments available to farmers who increased production. By 1945, 122 billion pounds of milk was being produced in the United States (Foote, 1947, p. 689).

Post War Adjustments

However, when the war ended, demand dropped but the dairy cows continued to produce milk at the rate they did during the war. Congress recognized that over-production had the potential of again creating economic hardship and in 1949 provided permanent authority for the Dairy Price Support Program first authorized by the Agricultural Adjustment Act of 1933.

The words "price support" can be deceiving because dairy farmers don't receive direct market or deficiency payments for producing milk like some crop farmers receive. The support program instead requires the Secretary of Agriculture provide a floor price for milk by guaranteeing that USDA's Commodity Credit Corporation (CCC) will buy unlimited quantities of storable dairy products (butter, cheddar cheese and non-fat dry milk) when the price reaches a "support price" level. This only occurs when milk supplies are greater than demand and milk prices fall.

Congress sets the support price level, and the Secretary of Agriculture, using make allowances and product yields similar to those now used in Federal Milk Marketing Orders, sets the price the government will pay manufacturers for cheese, nonfat dry milk and butter. In an attempt to reduce government expenditures for the program, since butter and nonfat dry milk are usually produced together and are considered to be joint products, the Secretary of Agriculture has authority to alter the prices of either product as long as the combined value of both stay at the announced CCC price. When this occurs, it is referred to as adjusting the butter/powder "tilt" because when one price goes up, the other must come down.

Since the support program doesn't guarantee producers a minimum price for their milk, the market price for manufacturing milk can fall below the announced support price. Milk processors may choose not to sell to the CCC because of the special packaging requirements, mandatory inspections, grading and delayed payment, making the cost of selling higher than to other commercial buyers. Product purchased by the program may be sold back to commercial markets at not less than the purchase price, or distributed to commodity feeding programs both in this country and abroad.

Technology's Role in the 1950s

With the introduction of the tractor, artificial insemination to improve genetics, the use of forage harvesters to produce silage, the milking machine, gutter cleaners and the bulk milk tank, farm productivity increased and farmers made the decision to either specialize in dairy farming or accept-off farm employment. With the investments in technology, farm debt mushroomed, but with wide-spread opportunities for public education, farmers were better equipped to make sound financial decisions.

Legislative Challenges

With the President and Congress involved in determining farm income through their authority to set prices in the farm bill, agriculture generally did fairly well, but each president found agriculture challenging. Erza Taft Benson, President Eisenhower's Secretary of Agriculture, spent eight years in office and was blamed for a record 3 million people leaving the farm. President Kennedy's campaign promise to guarantee 90 percent parity was broken. President Johnson focused the country on exporting its surplus products when consumers, concerned over cholesterol and strontium 90, reduced their consumption of dairy products.

Changing the Pricing Formulas To Reflect the Times

With the improvements in transportation systems and rapid expansion of the interstate highway system in the 1950s, milk began moving longer distances allowing butter, cheese and non-fat dry milk to be marketed nationally. It became necessary to begin pricing milk nationally as well, with the Minnesota Wisconsin or M-W price adopted in 1961 as the base price for manufacturing or Class III (cheese) products and "mover" for Class I (fluid) and Class II products, which are soft products usually eaten with a spoon. (A mover is a base price that is used to determine other prices.) Under the M-W formula, the Class I price was determined by adding a transportation differential that represented the cost of moving milk to the consumer from Eau Claire, Wisconsin. (See Appendix A for information on how the M-W price was calculated.)

Golden Age of Parity

When Richard Nixon became president, his efforts to control wages and prices suspended import quotas and led to a drop in milk prices. In the early 1970s, inflation pressure and a growing export market led to increased production. After President Jimmy Carter instituted a grain embargo against the Soviet Union in 1975, Congress raised the minimum support level to 80 percent of parity with semi-annual adjustments.

With assurances of higher milk prices, farmers responded by securing credit and investing the two years it takes to raise heifer calves into producing cows, creating a huge milk surplus. Government costs totaled more than $2.4 billion in 1981. In addition, the net government removals of butter accounted for nearly 75 percent of the total production, resulting in pressure to cut spending on CCC purchases. From its enactment until 1981, Congress gave the Secretary of Agriculture discretion in setting the support price to a range of 75 to 90 percent of the "parity price." The Agriculture and Food Act of 1981 (Farm Bill) departed from the traditional parity basis for supporting milk prices, and set the support price at $13.10 per hundred pounds (cwt)[3]. But over-production continued, and at the peak in 1983, government surplus acquisitions represented about 12 percent of all U.S. milk output (LaFrance, 2003).

In an attempt to bring production in line with consumption, a temporary Milk Diversion Program (MDP) was implemented from January 1, 1984 to March 31, 1985. The MDP paid dairy farmers $10 for every hundred pounds of milk that they voluntarily reduced from their base period, provided their reduction was between 5 and 30 percent below their base marketing levels. The program was financed by a $.50 per hundredweight assessment against all milk marketed. The program succeeded in reducing production from 139.6 billion pounds in 1983 to 135.4 billion in 1984, but once the program ended, production expanded again (Lee and Boisvert, 1985). The 1983 Dairy and Tobacco Adjustment Act began a process of lowering the support price to $10.10 per hundred pounds, which was accomplished in 1995.

The history of the support program can provide the country with valuable lessons on the dangers of setting milk prices artificially high enough to stimulate over production of milk without meaningful production controls. According to Wisconsin dairy economists Ed Jesse and Bob Cropp, high support prices in the late 1970s and early 80s "created a surplus situation that took 10 years to rectify." If the prices are too high, they can also distort markets and the allocation of milk between markets (Jesse and Cropp, 2004). This happened during much of the 1980s, when the CCC was the primary market outlet for nonfat dry milk. Much nonfat dry milk use was displaced by whey solids and imported casein, both of which were a cheaper source of milk protein. When companies change their formulas to use these alternative products, it is extremely difficult to have them change back, meaning some important markets can be permanently lost.

Cooperatives Remain Major Players in Supporting New England Farmers

Spurred on by milk prices below the cost of production, in 1973, eight Northeast cooperatives formed the federated Regional Cooperative Marketing Agency, Inc. (RCMA) to obtain prices that exceeded the minimum Federal Order price or over-order premiums. For eighteen months, from September 1973 to August 1975, the organization was somewhat successful, but there were too many independent producers to maintain the program.

In an effort to raise prices uniformly, the program was restructured to include farmers who were not cooperative members, allowing the association to control 90 percent of the milk and pay producer premiums for a period of 22 months, beginning in September 1987 in both the New York-New Jersey and New England Order Markets. While the program eventually collapsed, the idea of over-order pricing arose again in the Northeast Dairy Compact (Jacobson and Wasserman, 1992, August, pp. 1-5).

The Government Tries To Stabilize Prices

With a guarantee of high milk prices, the country was swimming in milk and the government was spending on average $2 billion a year to purchase approximately 12 billion pounds of excess dairy products (Short, 1989, p.1).

Looking for ways to further reduce production, the 1985 Farm Bill authorized the voluntary Dairy Termination Program (DTP). From April, 1986, to August, 1987, farmers were able to submit bids for the amount of money per hundred pounds they were willing to accept to cease milk production for at least five years, by slaughtering or exporting all their dairy cattle. Almost 14,000 bids were accepted, amounting to 12.3 million pounds of milk, equivalent to 8.7 percent of the milk leaving the market. However, this program didn't significantly reduce milk supply. It took lower support prices and a major drought in 1988 to bring production and consumption back into alignment.

Entering the 90s

The 1996 Farm Bill implemented a schedule to eliminate the support purchase program and replace it with a processor recourse loan program effective on December 31, 1999. However, with milk prices plummeting, subsequent legislation delayed the termination, and in the 2002 Farm Bill legislation reauthorized the support program at $9.90 for milk averaging 3.67 percent butterfat through December 31, 2007. At this level the support price is well below the cost of production, but the program can be important because in times of low prices, guaranteed CCC purchases count toward sales that are used to determine the Federal Order milk price.

By the 1990s, the majority of farmers were no longer producing Grade B milk, reducing both the number of plants available that could be surveyed and the reliability of the pricing information available to determine the milk value used in cheese production. Developing a new pricing method proved challenging. Finally in 1995, after numerous studies of alternatives, the M-W price was replaced with a temporary pricing program known as Basic Formula Price (BFP). The BFP continued to conduct surveys to determine the value of the milk used in cheese, but started using a product formula that adjusted the M-W price for changes in the wholesale prices of butter, cheese and nonfat dry milk (Collins, 2006).

The BFP formula was a band-aid until major Federal Order reform. Congress, in the Federal Agriculture Improvement and Reform Act of 1996 (Farm Bill), directed the Secretary of Agriculture to develop a new milk pricing formula and to reduce the number of Federal Milk Market Orders (FMMOs) within specific time frames. As USDA developed proposals to meet the Congressional mandate, "Order Reform" became the hot topic at dairy farmer gatherings.

Low Dairy Prices Again

Low milk prices, El Nino-driven storms and other natural disasters in 1998 resulted in Congress appropriating $200 million for direct payments to dairy producers and an additional $125 million in direct payments in 1999. To provide meaningful assistance to small and medium-sized dairy producers, USDA limited payments to each operation's first 26,000 hundredweight of milk production. This limit on eligible production capped payments on farms having approximately 150 or fewer cows, or about 13 percent of all farms (Chite, 1999).

Northeast Order Dairy Compact

After a decade of meetings, research and discussion and with strong cooperative support, the Northeast Order Dairy Compact was enacted by each of the New England states' legislature, approved by the Congress and signed by President Bill Clinton in 1996. This allowed Connecticut, Maine, Massachusetts, New Hampshire, Rhode Island and Vermont to set up a special pricing system for Class I milk that guaranteed a "safety net" or guaranteed minimum price of $1.46 a gallon (a price determined to be the minimum cost of production), for all of the Class 1 milk produced.

A board of farmers, retailers and processors representing each state administered the program that paid farmers $146 million (Ring, 2001) over its lifetime by requiring processors to pay a Compact Premium when the Federal Order Class I price fell below the Compact Class I target price of $16.94. Premiums were pooled in the Compact region's producer settlement pool and distributed back to eligible farmers.

Nationally, the Northeast Order Dairy Compact was politically divisive. While many other states wanted to create compacts in their region and the Northeast delegations in the U.S. House and Senate strongly supported its continuation, but after Sept. 11, 2001, the country wasn't focused on dairy legislation. New England dairy farmers, who control 1.3 million acres of open space (Ring, 2001), were unable to plan with certainty that their returns covered the costs of production and investment, and many went out of business since the expiration of the Compact on Sept. 30, 2001. The loss of these farms impacts the economic vitality, character and environment of our area.

Cooperatives Change to Meet Changing Demands

Cooperatives have also grown and changed. New England Milk Producers eventually merged with another cooperative, Connecticut Milk Producers, to form Yankee Milk. This cooperative dissolved in 1980 when members voted to create Agri-Mark and acquire the HP Hood processing plants, which were leased back to Hood, then a wholly-owned subsidiary of Agway. In 1989 Agri-Mark withdrew from the Hood Company, and in 1992, Cabot Creamery and Agri-Mark merged (Duffey, 2000) giving the cooperative the capacity to process up to 1.5 billion pounds annually (Wellington, 2006). They owned dairy processing facilities in West Springfield, MA, the Cabot (cheese) Creamery plant in Cabot, VT, the former Kraft plant in Middlebury, VT, and the McCadam cheese plant in Chateaugay, NY. Meanwhile, St. Albans Cooperative, now the largest dairy cooperative in Vermont, was processing and marketing over three million pounds of milk each day from approximately 516 members, supplying milk to many accounts, including Ben & Jerry's.

Dairylea, another well-known dairy cooperative, began at the urging of the New York State Grange as Dairymen's League in 1907, with the agreement it wouldn't function until it "secured members owning 50,000 cows," reached in 1910 (Selitzer, 1976, pp. 327-328). In 1999, Dairylea, in conjunction with Dairy Farmers of America's Northeast Area Council, formed Dairy Marketing Services, LLC (DMS), which manages the sale and distribution of the raw milk of both organizations.

Since its inception, DMS has taken on milk marketing for nearly 2,100 independent producers and 20 regional/local cooperatives, including St. Albans Cooperative. Most recently, the organization expanded its operations nationally. DMS' major customers include Kraft Foods, Saputo, Sorrento Cheese, Dean Foods, Leprino Foods, Great Lakes Cheese, HP Hood, and other smaller fluid and manufacturing customers.

Proprietary handler companies like HP Hood also expanded their operations by acquiring the Turner Center Systems in 1929, that operated creameries in Maine and New Hampshire, and store and city receiving plants in Boston, Lynn, Lowell, Lawrence, Worcester, and Fall River MA; and Providence, RI (Barnhart, 1947, p.24). In 1995, the Hood family sold their company to John Kaneb who created HP Hood, Inc. Kaneb expanded the company, buying Booth Brothers in Vermont and Crowley Foods in New Hampshire. Hood also produces Stonyfield Farm branded organic milk and Hannaford brand milk. Hood now can be found in dairy cases across the nation.

Today's cooperatives are part of a highly concentrated fluid milk processing industry and mega retailers are flexing their muscle and dictating the prices paid to suppliers. The ratio of dairy farmers to fluid milk processors remains high, milk is still a perishable product that can't be withheld from the market in an effort to gain a better price and there continues to be a problem finding a home for all the milk produced at certain times of the year. The United States doesn't have a quota system (except in California), so farmers can market all the milk they produce as long as it meets the quality standards.

The 1930s' Federal Milk Marketing Order, 70 Years Later

Over the years, the agricultural sector has changed. Initially, payments were made for milk not by hundredweight but by the gallon or 10-gallon can. Adapting to technology, farmers started using milking equipment that prevented humans from touching milk on its journey from the cow to the consumer. Better refrigeration throughout the entire marketing chain also improved milk quality. Dairy farming today requires the use of computers, land conservation techniques, financial management, business plans and a $2-3 million investment to operate a medium size farm.

In the Northeast, approximately 45 percent of the milk produced is bottled or used as beverage or fluid milk, but the demand for that milk varies. Seasonal events, holidays, the opening or ending of school and school vacations, as well as weather forecasts of storms, can create spikes or reductions in milk demand. New England also has a national reputation for producing quality cheese, ice cream and butter that consumers want to be able to buy on an as-needed basis.

To meet these demands, the FMMO program continues to play a role in the pricing of milk through classification and pooling. FMMO staff also conducts audits to ensure that all milk in the system is properly accounted. They also compile and release information on the number of producers and plants and volume of milk produced on a monthly basis. The Order also doesn't allow retail outlets to force farm prices below the minimum price set by the Market Administrator.

New Federal Order (Northeast Market Area Language)

Following a farmer referendum, in August, 1999, USDA announced farmers had approved amendments to reduce the number of Orders and a new pricing formula. Following some legal challenges, Congress passed and President Clinton signed the Consolidated Appropriations Act of 2000, which contained a provision allowing the new Order provisions to go into effect on January 1, 2000. (See Appendix B for a comparison between the BFP and new pricing provisions.)

The new Order reduced the number of FMMOs to 11 and eventually 10 when the Western Order was terminated in 2004. In the Northeast, former Federal Order 1 (New England), Order 2 (New York-New Jersey) and Order 4 (Mid-Atlantic) were combined into a new order called Federal Milk Order 1-Northeast Marketing Area. The new order that encompasses a 97,000 square mile area includes all the New England states except Maine, the states of Delaware, New Jersey, and the District of Columbia, parts of New York, Pennsylvania, Virginia and Maryland. According to the Milk Market Administrator's Bulletin in January 2007, a total of 13,901 farmers or producers were pooled under the Order with the farmers producing on average 4,361 pounds or 500 gallons of milk per day (The Market Administrator's Bulletin, Northeast Marketing Area, 2007, January).

While 500 gallons a day can sound like a great deal of milk, statistics from 2003, illustrate how small farms here are compared to farmers in the Southwest Order who produced 3,364 gallons a day. In the Arizona - Las Vegas Order the production per farm per day was 9,200 gallons (The Market Administrator's Bulletin, Northeast Marketing Area, 2006, February). These farms are located in an area where a favorable climate for milk production, lower production costs, ample supplies of good quality forage and innovations in technology create an environment that encourages milk production that has a competitive advantage over the farmers on small farms located in New England.

Pricing Milk

Until the 1890s, dishonest farmers would adulterate, water down or remove some cream from their milk before they sold it because milk was priced by volume only. That changed when Stephen Babcock from the University of Wisconsin developed the Babcock test that was able to measure the butterfat content in milk. Farmers began to be paid on the fat content and a butterfat differential based on milk testing at 3.5 percent fat, which encouraged them to produce milk with a higher fat content.

For the next 100 years milk was priced based on both volume and butterfat. However, today society is changing. With numerous beverage choices, people are not choosing milk to be the beverage at each meal. Concerns about fat have reduced the amount of milk used for butter manufacturing and a love for cheese has dramatically increased the volume used in making all types of cheese, while ice cream consumption has stayed about level. The new Order language recognized these changes when it placed a value on all of the components - butterfat, protein, and other solids in milk by adopting a "Multiple Component Pricing" (MCP) formula. Normally the total value of all the milk produced exceeds this value, and farmers are paid a bonus or producer price differential, abbreviated PPD, which is a measure of value of their milk in excess of the Class III component value. However, when milk prices are moving rapidly, the Order will not have enough money to pay a positive PPD.

By using formulas and having information on pricing and production trends available on their websites or by email, the new Order provisions make it easier to forecast prices and provides more transparency to the price-setting process. It is also creating more volatility in milk prices. Average Class I milk price averages sprang from $13.86 per one hundred pounds in 2004, to $17.84 in 2005, and back to $15.13 in 2006 (The Market Administrator's Bulletin, Northeast Marketing Area, 2007, January). In July of 2007, it reached a then-record high of $24.16 or $2.07 a gallon compared to the July 2006, when the price was $14.59 or $1.25 a gallon (The Market Administrator's Bulletin, Northeast Marketing Area, 2007, July).

The New Formulas Have Some Familiarity

The basic tenant of milk pricing since the 1930s - setting minimum prices, classifying milk according to use and revenue pooling, remain in the new order provisions. Now there are four classes of milk, with the same prices across the country for all but Class I or beverage milk, priced to reflect the higher cost associated with supplying the fluid market. (See Appendix C for a description of the Classes and the pricing formulas.) The new Order boundaries provide incentives for greater structural efficiencies in the assembly and shipment of milk for fluid milk products, while maintaining equity among processors and the dairy farmers in the marketing order areas.

With Multiple Component Pricing, the new formula-based procedure is used for setting minimum class prices that tie all Federal Order milk prices to the wholesale prices of Grade AA butter, cheddar cheese, nonfat dry milk and dry whey. Every week the National Agricultural Statistics Service (NASS) surveys qualified plants to determine the wholesale prices of specific dairy products. The results are plugged into formulas that derive the values of the components. Then these numbers are adjusted for the cost of manufacturing (or a make allowance), and the average number of pounds of product made from the component. For example, the value of butterfat will be determined based on the price of butter, less the cost of manufacturing, multiplied by the number of pounds of butter that can be made from a pound of butterfat.

Each Federal Market Administrator's office announces prices twice a month, with the first announcement on a Friday before the 23rd of the month, before production occurs, for the prices for Class I skim milk and butterfat and Class II skim milk. These prices are determined from two weeks of NASS surveys. The second price announcement occurs on a Friday before the 5th of the month following production, for milk used in Class III cheese, Class IV nonfat dry milk and whey products, and the Class II butterfat price.

These values are then used to determine the price of Class III (cheese) and Class IV (nonfat dry milk and whey) products. Once these prices are known, a location-specific differential is added to the price mover (the higher of the Class III or Class IV price) to set the Class I price for beverage milk. The price of Class II products, usually eaten by a spoon (ice cream, yogurt, etc.) is equal to the Class IV price plus $0.70. (See Appendix C for a further description of how the pricing is determined.)

Once the final prices for raw milk are known, then the pooling process begins. Every milk dealer/processor and cooperative that meet the qualifications to participate in the Federal Market Order program must report the amount of milk they purchased and how it was utilized in the Northeast Marketing Order to the Milk Market Administrator on or before the 10th of every month. The office then determines the value of the pool, which represents the total volume of milk used in each of the four classes, times the respective price for each class.

After the total value of all the milk is determined, the Statistical Uniform Price (SUP), similar to the blend price used prior to 2000, is announced for milk that contains 3.5 percent butterfat, 2.99 percent protein and 5.69 percent other solids, delivered to Suffolk County, MA (Boston), the base pricing point for the Northeast Federal Order. The SUP price is always given on a hundred pound basis and equals the Class III price plus the PPD price.

As part of the pooling process, the Market Administrator's office determines each milk plant's portion of the pool by calculating the weighted-average value of milk used by each pooled plant and applying the announced Class prices to the volume of milk used by the plant in each class. Milk plants that have the calculated value of their milk greater than the average weighted-average for the entire pool (this would be plants that primarily package beverage milk) are billed for the difference between the average market value multiplied by the plant's producer deliveries for the month. Since the plant knows in advance what the value of this milk is and undoubtedly set the price they sold their milk based on that, they have money available to pay into the Producer Settlement Fund.

On the other hand, a plant with a weighted-average milk value of less than the market value, because they primarily make manufactured products, receives a check for the difference in value times the pounds of milk they used from the Producer Settlement Fund. Through these Producer Settlement Fund pay-ins and take-outs, each pooled plant has the same amount of money per hundredweight to pay farmers the minimum announced Federal Order price at the plant where they shipped their milk, regardless of what products the plant makes. During this process, milk dealers also are assessed their share of the costs to administer the Order. (See Appendix D for further information on payments to the Producer Settlement Fund.)

Pumping milk from the bulk tank to the tank truck at the Crete Farm, Boscawen, NH.

Farmers' Milk Price

With the pooling and payments complete, it's time to follow the money to the farmers who produce the milk. While they may follow the price announcements to determine how much money is available to pay them, their pricing is based on different formulas.

Each time a farmer's milk goes to market, the milk truck driver records the amount of milk in the bulk tank and takes a sample that is delivered to a laboratory to monitor compliance with quality standards, ensure no antibiotics are present in milk and determine the components (protein, butterfat, milk solids). This information is used to calculate the farmer's minimum Multiple Component Price payment plus the Producer Price Differential. (To learn how a farmer finds these prices, review the Federal Milk Marketing Order Price Announcement which is in Appendix E.)

Ken Leroux, DFA truck driver, is shown sampling milk at the Crete Farm, Boscawen, NH.

As an example, a farmer produces milk at the announced multiple component values of 3.5 percent butterfat, 2.99 percent protein and 5.59 percent other solids. The milk check is determined first by establishing component values by:

- Announced butterfat price multiplied by 3.5 percent.

- Plus the announced protein price multiplied by 2.99 percent.

- Plus the announced other solids price multiplied by 5.99 percent.

When these figures are totaled, the Class III price or total component value has been determined. However, since farmers also are paid on the volume of milk they produce (and in the Market Administrator's total pool there is usually money available to pay farmers for this), the value of Class I, II, and IV milk sent to market needs to be determined. This is done by subtracting the total component value at Class III prices from the total classified value, which is the value of Class I, Class II and Class IV components listed on the Pool Price Announcement of all the milk in the pool, subtracting a small portion for the Producer Settlement Fund Reserve, and dividing this net value by the total amount of farmers' milk in the pool. When this is completed, the PPD is announced. The PPD and Class III price when combined always equal the statistical uniform price.

Most of the time, the relationship between Class III price and PPD is an inverse relationship. However, there are times when the Class III price is rapidly rising and there is a negative PPD because the statistical uniform price for the month is less than the Class III price. When this happens, farmers are paid more for Class III components than the entire blend pool is worth. In this situation, it is important to note that because the value of butterfat, protein, and other solids increased, the farmer's overall price is a higher price even if the resulting PPD is negative. The PPD is one way farmers are rewarded for producing milk in a region with relatively high Class I use such as the Northeast. (For more information on farm calculations view Appendix E.)

Farmers actually receive two milk checks during the month. On or before 26th day of the month, dairy producers are paid a "partial payment" for the milk shipped from their farms during the first 15 days of the month. The partial payment price is based on the lowest class price from the previous month. The final payment paid to producers is for the milk produced between the 16th and the end of the month, minus the partial payment. Thus, the final payment price is equal to the SUP or blend price minus the partial payment.

The actual amount of money farmers receive for their milk can vary. Farmers pay to haul their milk to the processing plant and that can cost an average New Hampshire dairy farmer $20,000 a year to send milk to the Boston market. However, since milk is priced based on the plant location, the Statistical Uniform Price and the PPD formulas use differentials in their formulas to provide higher prices for milk delivered to plants closer to Suffolk County, MA (Boston), the pricing point for the Northeast Federal Order. According to the Federal Milk Market Order, May 2007 price report, the SUP for milk delivered to Boston was $18.60, while the price for milk delivered to a plant in St. Albans, VT was $17.75. (See Appendix F for a Chart of Differentials.)

The FMMO only establishes minimum prices. (See Appendix G for details about the functions of Federal Orders.) Farmers may see premium payments in their milk check for quality, the volume of their milk or competitive payments for market conditions. Dairy farmers who are transitioning or producing organic milk sign a contract to be paid an additional amount per hundredweight for the extra value that organic milk returns from the marketplace. Counter-cyclical payments from programs like the Milk Income Loss Contract (MILC) are added to the final price farmers are paid.

Most milk checks also contain additional deductions besides the costs of milk hauling and stop charges. Cooperative members may see deductions for membership dues and equity payments used to fund member-owned processing plants and equipment. In addition, all farmers pay 15 cents per hundredweight for a generic milk promotion program through a dairy check-off program and may pay ten cents per hundredweight to a program known as Cooperatives Working Together (CWT) to help balance nationwide milk supplies.

Other programs that impact the price farmers receive today for their milk

Milk Protein Concentrate (MPC)

A milk filtration process was developed in the 1970s to filter protein from milk. The result of this process is products that food labels refer to as milk protein concentrates (MPCs)-wet ultra-filtered (UF) milk protein products, casein and caseinates.

Many foreign countries are producing MPC, and since 1990, processors in the United States began importing them. A May, 2004, report, *Conditions of Competition for Milk Protein Products in the U.S. Market* (Coleman, J., et al., 2004, May) submitted by an independent, nonpartisan, fact-finding federal agency, the International Trade Commission (ITC), confirms these imports may have displaced 318 million pounds (on a protein basis) of U.S.-produced milk protein products over the 1998-2002 period. The same reports states "MPC purchases are dominated by two end-use applications: processed cheese products (62 percent) and specialty nutrition products (24 percent)."

Because many products aren't regulated under the tariffs or quota provisions in the existing World Trade Organization agreements, Congress is trying to determine how to treat them. The largest milk cooperative organization, the National Milk Producers Federation (NMPF), is urging Congress to examine provisions in the Trade Act of 1974.

This Trade Act allows the President (following an International Trade Commission investigation) to provide relief to a U.S. industry adversely affected by imports by allowing the U.S. Trade Representative to retaliate against certain foreign trade policies, and use anti-dumping laws and countervailing measures (Galen, 2001). On the other side of the issue are dairy manufactures like International Dairy Foods Association that contend MPC imports can't be substituted by non-fat dry milk and the domestic support price for nonfat dry milk should be reduced to create incentives for MPC production in the United States.

Milk Income Loss Contract (MILC)

The Milk Income Loss Contract (MILC) is a counter-cyclical program added to the already complicated mix of federal dairy programs in the 2002 Farm Bill retroactive to 2001. Many saw its adoption as an alternative to continuing and expanding regional dairy compacts. The national program provides farmers with a certain amount of income protection by requiring the federal government make payments to eligible farmers when the announced Federal Order price for Class I drops below $16.94 per hundred pounds at Suffolk County (Boston).

Unlike the Northeast Order Dairy Compact that authorized payments to New England dairy farmers from the milk dealers when the price of milk dropped below $16.94, MILC payments come from the federal government. Farmers are only eligible to receive a payment on 2.4 million pounds of production in a fiscal year (roughly the amount of milk produced on a 120-cow dairy farm).

In the original legislation, payments were equal to 45 percent of the difference between the $16.94 per hundred pounds target price and the market price in any month the Boston price falls below the target. When the MILC expired in September, 2004, as milk prices fell, there was a great deal of concern for the small family farm. On February 8, 2006, Congress, in the Deficit Reduction Act of 2005, authorized an extension of the program, referred to as MILCX, through August, 2007.

However, as a cost-saving measure aimed at keeping the total cost of the program under $1 billion, the payment rate was reduced from 45 percent to 34 percent of the difference in price.

Cooperatives Working Together (CWT)

Cooperatives Working Together (CWT) has joined approximately 70 percent of the farmers in the United States together in a program that assesses dairy producers 10 cents per hundred pounds of milk sold, with the money used to reduce the imbalances between supply and demand that can lead to lower milk prices. The program provides an incentive to dairy manufacturers and exporters to sell to foreign, commercial markets and reduces milk production by purchasing whole herds of cows.

Dairy Export Incentive Program (DEIP)

In 2006, 9.3 percent, or an equivalent basis 2.092 billion pounds of milk produced in the United States, was exported (Dryer, 2007), indicating the Dairy Export Incentive Program (DEIP) is another important component of the dairy farm support programs. In a global market, United States dairy goods must compete with highly subsidized products, particularly those produced by the European Union. To help level the playing field, Congress authorized the CCC in 1985 to pay cash bonuses to U.S. exporters of cheese, non-fat dry milk and butter. Both the total quantities exported and the total budgetary expenditures are subject to limits imposed by commitments with the World Trade Organization.

Cabot Creamery gives this program credit with helping them introduce aged cheddar cheese in England in 1997 (Business Wire, 1997).

Dairy Futures and Options

In the 2002 Farm Bill, a pilot program was funded to encourage farmers to reduce their risks by trading in dairy futures and options contracts. Futures contracts are standardized, legally- binding agreements to buy or sell a specific product or financial instrument in the future. For dairy producers the contract is an agreement between them or their cooperatives and a milk dealer to purchase a certain amount of milk used for non-fluid products for a defined period of time.

By entering into a forward contract with a dealer, a dairy farmer gives up the right to receive the minimum Federal Order prices for the amount of their milk under contract. Based on the results of the pilot program, future farm legislation may contain incentives to farmers to consider futures trading as a risk management strategy (USDA/AMS, 2002, p. 5).

Opposition appears to be growing to the ideas of making the pilot forward contracting permanent, because unlike other commodities, milk priced under the Federal Milk Marketing Order program already guarantees a farmer a minimum price, and there is concern this protection will be lost. Opponents also point out to farmers and dairy processors interested in the program, they are already allowed to use options on the Chicago Mercantile Exchange (Farmshine, 2007, p. 13).

Farmers and Processors Make Investment in Promotion

Since 1980, milk produced per cow has risen by an average of 2.1 percent yearly, while milk consumption (in all products) over the same time period increased by an average of only 1.4

percent. Recognizing the need to compete with other beverages for the consumer's marketing dollar, in 1983 Congress authorized mandatory assessments on all U.S. dairy farmers and the fluid milk handlers to fund milk promotion activities.

According to Lloyd Day, USDA Administrator of Ag Marketing Services, in 2005, farmers contributed more than $260 million and processors contributed about $105 million spent on promotion to increase the consumer demand for dairy products. The newly introduced single-serving milk bottle used in schools and restaurants is expected to add over a billion pounds of milk to fluid sales (Day, 2006). The "Three Servings-A-Day" and "Got Milk" campaigns and National Dairy Council efforts that bring nutrition education into schools and health institutions are also funded with promotion funds.

The Future

Great advances have occurred in the dairy industry. While there are only 230,000 cows in New England, they produced milk valued at $686,098,000 in 2005 (NASS, 2007). After years of competing for the consumer beverage dollar with the soda industry, bottled water is surpassing milk in sales. Organic milk sales are growing and consumer consumption of low fat dairy products is increasing.

Over production that drives down prices continues to plague the industry, but there appears to be recognition on the part of elected officials that dairy farms are important to the local economy and for the environment. In 2006 and 2007, most New England state governments voted to provide payments to farmers to support them during a period of extremely low prices. The money was very helpful as farmers wrestled with higher feed bills, because corn had been diverted from animal feed to bio-fuel, which raised the cost of this common ingredient in cattle feed.

As we look to the future, international demand for dairy products will open new markets and prop up domestic prices. With a history of innovation and dedication, New England dairy farmers will continue to meet the challenges of producing nature's most nearly perfect food.

(Footnotes)

[1] Around 1830, dairies were established next to distilleries and in New York City cows were fed distillery slop, while in Boston they were fed brewer's grain, leading to the production of milk that was very thin and a pale bluish color, adulterated by adding starch, sugar, flour, plaster of Paris, eggs, etc. This milk was blamed for causing many fatal diseases in young children.

[2] A bulk tank is a refrigerated, stainless steel storage tank located at the dairy, designed to hold milk as soon as it leaves the cow. The milk is cooled immediately in the bulk tank, usually to 35-39 degrees F. The milk is then collected by a bulk tank truck and shipped to a processing plant. Initial tanks required a $3,000 to $5,000 investment.

[3] Milk weights are always in pounds or hundredweights (cwt) with one cwt, being equivalent to 11.63 gallons

The Grange served an important function in the farming community lobbying for legislation to benefit agriculture and serving as an important social organization for rural residents.

The Grange, represented in a parade, possibly at the Eastern States Exposition in West Springfield, MA. Left to right are Wesley Adams, Derry, unknown, George R. Drake, Manchester, Fred Rogers, Meridan, Charlie Varney, unknown

(Adams Farm - Westmoreland, NH)
Well-groomed farmsteads provide the rural atmosphere and scenic views that tourists enjoy when taking rides through the country. The open space created by farming activities also provides the setting desired by those who choose to retire or have second homes in New Hampshire.

Quality of Life, Agritourism and Ecological Value

The quality of life that makes New Hampshire a desirable place to live and visit is linked to green space, scenic views and the historical and cultural values dairy farmers provide. These values help recruit businesses, become the basis for recreation and tourism and are invoked as "the New Hampshire Advantage," yet taken for granted until a town loses its last farm (Resource Systems Group, 1999, p. 11).

New Hampshire's dairy industry delivers positive impacts beyond those attributable to its direct financial contribution to the state's economy. Because the social and environmental impacts of the New Hampshire dairy industry are difficult to measure, they are often overlooked. Dairy farmers are the stewards of 83,365 acres of cropland and forest that maintain open space(U.S. Census, New Hampshire, 2002, p. 133). These farmers have a long-term commitment to their working landscapes. If the fields and orchards were left untended, brush would grow into trees and block many scenic vistas. Since the average dairy farm is in excess of 430 total acres (U.S. Census, New Hampshire, 2002, p. 133), decisions by dairy farmers to leave the business can lead to sizable land use changes and loss of these generally unmeasured and overlooked indirect benefits.

Rural Character and Measurable Economic Values of Open Space

New Hampshire has been the fastest growing state in the entire northeast for the past 40 years and is expected to continue in that pattern for the foreseeable future (NH Changing Landscapes, 2005, p 1). Not only is the state growing rapidly, but more land is used per person than in earlier years (Achieving Smart Growth in New Hampshire, 2003, p. 1). As growth and development increasingly change the visual appearance of many New Hampshire communities, open space and scenic views become more precious resources. Master Plans of several New Hampshire communities express the desire of the townspeople to "retain its rural character," and many of the people who choose to move to the state or have seasonal homes here are drawn by the desirable rural character. Volunteer planning boards and professional planners alike struggle to find tools that balance the need for development to accommodate the growing population and the desire to retain what people love most about their communities.

Unfortunately for the future of agriculture in the state, the land most suitable for farming is often the easiest and most desirable to develop. Some cities and towns are starting to become possessive of their last remaining farms, understanding their importance in preserving open space and providing the benefit of fresh, locally grown food.

However, the need for new houses and commercial land uses continues to rise. The value of farmland for developed use is so high compared to the income that can be generated from farming that it is harder and harder for farm families to continue with the historical use of farming. Many operating farms also rent or lease additional land from nearby landowners, increasing the number of acres that are kept in productive, open space uses. Because of the link between a prosperous agricultural economy and retaining land in open space, a state policy of providing financial incentives to farmers is one way to encourage the preservation of open space.

Farmland is often desirable for development such as the Daniel Webster Farm in West Franklin, NH.

In a further effort to maintain open space, New Hampshire has had several programs to purchase conservation easements on farmland ensuring that it is kept in farming in perpetuity. Unfortunately there is not enough money to protect all the desirable land. Dairy farmers, especially those close to retirement, may often be discouraged with low milk prices and sell for top dollar to a developer. Other times farmers who depend on rented property to sustain their operations find that when owners of that rented land choose to sell their land, the farmer can't compete with the price developers are willing to pay, and they lose much needed cropland.

With the increased concern about the loss of open space, the Society for the Protection of New Hampshire Forests requested the Resource System Group to develop an economic analysis of the impact of open space on the economy of New Hampshire. The purpose of the study was to provide a factual basis for informing the public and policy makers about the value of open space. Open space was defined as areas that are not built-up, excavated, or developed (Resource Systems Group, 1999, p.1).

The Resource System Group study related open space directly to four economic sectors: agriculture, forestry, tourism and recreation, and second homes. The study recognized that there were economic contributions to the state's economy which couldn't be qualified with available data, including the value of open space in making New Hampshire an attractive place to live and to attract and retain business and industry (Resource Systems Group, 1999, p.1). The study used available data from a variety of state and federal government sources in an input/output model to quantify the value of open space. The economic impacts of open space are summarized in Table 1.

Table 1.

Summary of the Economic Impacts Related to Open Space Activities in New Hampshire 1996/97

	Gross Direct Income	Average Percent Attributed to Open Space	Attributed Direct Income	Attributed Direct Jobs	Attributed Direct & Indirect Income	Attributed Direct & Indirect Jobs	Attributed State & Local Tax Revenues
Agriculture	$413,400,000	56%	$230,900,000	3,669	$376,915,800	5,467	$30,907,096
Related Forest	$1,198,214,000	100%	$1,198,214,000	6,487	$3,921,182,894	16,675	$325,300,797
Related Tourism & Recreation	$3,178,480,000	54%	$1,732,261,600	41,661	$3,067,152,265	64,002	$249,417,502
Vacation Homes	$478,783,000	100%	$478,783,000	8,648	$816,983,565	15,029	$285,855,786
Total	$5,268,877,000	69%	$3,640,158,600	60,465	$8,182,234,524	101,173	$891,481,182

(Source: Resource Systems Group, 1999, p.15).

The study also found that open space related activities employ 16 percent of the state's work force, yield 25 percent of the gross state product and deliver 35 percent of total state and local tax revenues. These figures make it clear that open space has a strong effect on the state's economy.

In addition there is the ripple effect on jobs, indirect income and state and local tax revenues when all sectors prosper. The 5,265,000 acres of land in New Hampshire that meet the definition of open space contribute an average of $1,500 per acre in total state income each year (Resource Systems Group, 1999, p. 16). Agriculture is an important element in these totals, further highlighting the economic benefit of this traditional land use.

Two other studies explored the relationship between property taxes and land use in all 234 municipalities in the state. The first study found that on average, tax bills are higher in towns with more taxable property value, more year-round residents and more commercial and industrial development. The same studies found that, on average, taxes are lower in towns with more open space, and with more vacation homes (Ad Hoc Associates, 1994, pp. 1-2). A second, more recent and detailed study, found that towns that have the most permanently protected land on average have slightly lower tax bills, while tax bills are higher in towns with more residents and or more buildings (Trust for Public Land, 2005, pp. 22- 23).

Open space has often been regarded by city and town officials as areas of potential loss of tax revenue compared to the property tax income that might be generated if it were converted to a more developed use. A number of recent studies have shed some new light on the economic value of open space lands. Cost of Community Services (COCS) studies have been carried out in 15 different New Hampshire communities by a variety of researchers, including the University of New Hampshire Cooperative Extension. The methodology for these studies was pioneered by the American Farmland Trust.

The COCS studies typically compare income and expense by land use type for a single year in a specific community. The land use types included are usually residential, commercial - industrial and open space. The analyses determine the ratio of income to expense for each land use type for the time period under study.

The Upper Connecticut River Valley has some of the best soils in the state, used to grow feed for dairy cattle. These fields yield 20-25 tons of corn silage per acre or 3-5 tons of dry hay per acre. These beautiful scenes, enjoyed from Route 10 in Haverhill, are only made possible by the cultivation of the land by the farmers. Shown above is the Conklin Farm's field in Haverhill, NH.

In every New Hampshire town studied so far, open space pays more in taxes than it requires in cost of services. For each dollar of revenue generated by open space, towns only had to provide $0.21 - $0.94 in services. On the other hand, in every case except one, the services required for residential land use cost more than the income generated by that land use type, by a range of $1.01 to $1.17 of cost per dollar of income. The single exception found so far was Alton, where residential properties require $0.92 in services for every dollar they generate in revenue. Alton has many high-value second homes that don't require year-round services. (See Table 2.)

Table 2.

Summary Cost of Community Services Study Results
Expense to Income Ratios for Residential and Open Space Land Uses

(Graph excerpted from slide presentation The Dollars and Sense of Saving Special Places, UNH Cooperative Extension and Center for Land Conservation Assistance/Society for the Protection of New Hampshire Forests, 2006)

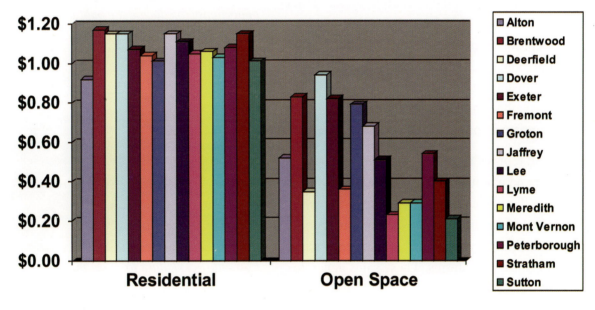

Lee is one of the towns that has done a Cost of Community Services Study, and has been aggressively seeking land conservation projects, largely in recognition of the natural resource benefits of conservation. It has been a pioneer in establishing an Agriculture Commission and the concept is being considered in other communities. Lee has focused especially on conserving working farmland. They have found additional benefits of open land that include:

- Water quality protection through infiltration and natural filtration
- Aquifer recharge
- Floodwater detention
- Wildlife habitat
- Scenic vistas (The Cost of Community Services, 2005, p.2).

The general pattern of many New Hampshire studies, as well as more than 60 similar studies conducted in other parts of the country, show that the income from residential property very rarely pays for services that the residents demand. Undeveloped open space requires fewer services and provides dollars to the town or city (Dollars and Sense of Saving Special Places slide show, 2006).

Agritourism

Agritourism, loosely defined as tourist activities that relate to the agricultural industry, is a growing component of the social and economic value of farms in New Hampshire. In 2002-2003 the NH Department of Agriculture, Markets & Food initiated a project with the Institute of New Hampshire Studies at Plymouth State University to look at the impact of agriculture on New Hampshire's economy, with a special emphasis on agritourism as part of the investigation. The report contained four sections: the economic impact of the state's eleven agricultural fairs; the dollar revenue from farm products purchased directly from farms, roadside markets and farm stands by tourists; the economic impact of tourists intentionally driving through agricultural areas to view the scenery; and the total tourism impacts related to agriculture.

Agricultural tourists make an estimated 520,000 trips and spend about $201 million each year, including $26 million for farm products. These products include a wide variety of farm produce including: milk, dairy foods and maple syrup from New Hampshire dairy farms. These sales generate jobs, rooms and meals taxes, fees, etc. Many tourists come to the state in part because they enjoy purchasing locally-produced agricultural products and other goods (Goss, 2003, p.9).

The report showed that $40.1 million is spent directly at fairs and the total impact of agricultural fairs was $106.4 million in transactions (Goss, 2003, p. 8). Animal agriculture is an important part of fairs, which differentiates them from carnivals. People enjoy watching the cows, horses, sheep dogs etc. in the show ring, and children like to see and pat the animals in their stalls.

New Hampshire's agriculture fairs generate over $106.4 million in revenue and are an opportunity to educate the public about agriculture.

Fairs attract visitors from neighboring states who spend money on goods and services.

Agriculture fairs are different from carnivals, as there are farm animals fitted and exhibited by 4-H'ers like Faith Putnam above, and commercial dairy farms. The three photos above are from the North Haverhill Fair.

The study by the Institute went beyond the direct value of purchased farm products to quantify the relationship between agriculture and tourist visits. The survey revealed:

- About 40 percent of all tourist and business travelers in the state are involved with outdoor recreation.

- About 30 percent of these are engaged in passive recreation, including scenic drives. If it is assumed that 20 percent of all passive recreation includes scenic drives through agricultural areas, then six percent of all visitors engage in this activity.

- Individuals took an estimated 1.6 million trips to view agricultural scenery and not purchase farm products, generating direct spending of $109 million related to the agricultural landscape. This had a ripple effect on employment, taxes, direct spending, etc., so that the total impact from agricultural related tourism was $282.4 million in transactions (Goss, 2003, pp. 10-11).

Agriculture tourists spend $26 million for farm products annually and appreciate buying the local New Hampshire flavor. Shown above is Dave Keith's farm stand, North Haverhill, NH.

Route 10 along the Connecticut River has many scenic vistas of operating farmland. Farm families along the way have opened farm stores and gift shops, such as the Round Barn Shoppe, owned by George and Ramona Schmid, Piermont, NH.

Commercial kitchens allow the production of relishes, pickles, condiments and baked goods that are sold to tourists and local residents. Shown above is the Robie Farm Kitchen, Piermont, NH.

Ecological Value

Even bigger than the common intangibles cited for farmland, such as quality of life and scenic vistas, are the "ecological services" or "natural capital" these working landscapes provide (Chichilnisky and Heal, 1998, p. 629). These terms describe the non-market values that open land itself contributes to the overall good of the life-supporting ecosystems and to human health and well being such as:

- Social and economic functions of ecosystem services,
- Purification of air and water,
- Mitigation of floods and droughts,
- Detoxification and decomposition of wastes,
- Generation and preservation of soils,
- Control of most potential agricultural pests,
- Pollination of crops and natural vegetation,
- Dispersal of seeds,
- Cycling of nutrients,
- Maintenance of biodiversity,
- Protection of coastal shores from erosion,
- Protection from harmful ultraviolet light,
- Partial stabilization of climate, and
- Provision of aesthetic beauty and intellectual stimulation. (Chichilinisky and Heal, 1998, p. 630)

Development of hillside farms causes a channeling of water run-off that needs to be controlled by rock ditches. The natural farmland mitigates this water flow over large expanses of gentle rolling fields.

As farmers produce food, they maintain open space as part of their daily cropping operations. Good management practices can minimize the negative impact farming practices might have on the land. Farming in itself keeps land open, provides a buffer among residential areas and is a useful and attractive alternative to development. This land also serves both to produce food and to provide ecological services that benefit all of society.

Global estimates of the value of ecological services annually exceed 33 trillion dollars; however, researchers say, "relatively few methods exist for pricing the multitudes of ecosystem services that constitute the earth's

Cropped farmland creates a separation from development.

life-support system" (Costanza, et. al., 1997, p. 259). There are soil organisms as well as flora and fauna that may be performing functions that aren't even discovered yet and contributing to ecological services. As these populations disappear, it affects the ability of ecosystems to function and may impact their resilience (Dasgupta, et. al., p. 343).

Gross Domestic Product (GDP) and other measures of conventional market economics look only at the production and consumption of purchased goods and services, but don't take into account the destruction of natural capital to accomplish it (Czech, 2003, pp. 1455-1456). If the price of purchased goods reflected the true costs of consumptive use of natural resources, cleaning up the resulting air and water pollution and disposing of wastes, measures of economic success might look quite different.

One attempt to measure true economic progress is the Genuine Progress Indicator (GPI). Costanza (2006, p. 26) describes this as "the estimate of the value of non-marketed goods and services provided by natural, human, and social capital and adjusts for income-distribution effects." Using this measure, what could look like a prosperous economy might actually be declining when all costs are included. Eventually the cost of liquidating natural capital needs to be reflected in prices, to steer the global economy and cause some action in correcting the consumption of natural resources (Hayes, 2004, pp. 1461-1462).

Research has shown that agricultural management enhances biodiversity and preserves some of these ecological services (although not always acknowledged by traditional ecologists). Low-intensity agriculture as practiced in the 19th century had less impact on the rural landscape (Tscharntke, et al., 2005, pp. 857-859). New Hampshire's farms of today are different than the large mega-farms of the western part of the country. Their practices are better alternatives to development to enhance biodiversity and ecosystem functions and provide more resources for animal and plant life. The role of farms in carbon sequestration, preserving watersheds and air filtration may make it practical to conserve land of marginal agricultural value (Chichilnisky and Heal, 1998, p. 629). In the past, land preservation was based largely on soil types and crop production potential, without valuing the ecological services of the land itself.

What happened in the mid-1990s to the New York City watershed offers a classic example of valuing ecological services of land. The city's water supply came from a watershed in the Hudson Valley and needed to be of good quality. The natural flow of water though the countryside, normally purified by root systems and soil microorganisms along the way, was contaminated by sewage, fertilizer and pesticides in the soil to the point where the water no longer met Environmental Protection Agency (EPA) quality standards (Nickens and Eddie, 1998, pp. 21-22).

The choices available to New York's water planners: build a filtration plant for $6 billion to $8 billion, with an annual operating cost of $300 million; or restore the watershed and all of its non-market eco-services, for $1 billion to $1.5 billion. In 1996, they invested in natural capital. They bought land within and around the watershed to restrict its uses. They subsidized improvements to sewer systems, built manure storage units on farms and took other actions that restored the ecological services (Chichilnisky and Heal, 1998, p. 629). For dairy farms, one solution to improve water quality and air contamination was to help them build anaerobic digesters for the manure. These would control odors, reduce pathogens and produce methane for heating the digester and generating electricity (Ludington and Weeks, 2006, p. 21).

The New York City water project put a real dollar value on natural services that had been taken for granted. It recognized that development stresses the ecological system.

Residential, commercial and industrial land uses all create issues of run-off, septic systems, road salt, lawn fertilizer and pesticides. For instance, water systems are likely to be contaminated by the five to ten pounds of pesticide per acre that typical home owners apply to maintain green lawns (Reifer, 2001, p. 67). Purchasing conservation easements that allow farming and forestry enterprises to operate under good management practices is one way to maintain the natural systems that help ensure a safe water supply for the region (Nickens and Eddie, 1998, p. 22).

Two methane digesters were built in New Hampshire during the 1970s, located in Claremont and Henniker. Those are no longer in existence, and the only one in the state is at the Fairchild Dairy Teaching and Research Center at UNH, shown above. It is currently in disrepair, but plans are being made to restore it to operation.

Not only do New Hampshire dairy farms supply fresh milk to the people of the state, but they contribute to the economy of the state and help to maintain the ecosystems that filter impurities, making New Hampshire a good place to live. Dairy farmers' responsible management of open space delivers millions of dollars worth of ecological services, which are not reflected in the economics of farming, the state's gross returns or the way our society values agricultural land. Dairy farmers help maintain the quality of life that is so precious to the residents of the state.

(Matt Tarr Photo)

Wildlife and Grassland Habitats

Pre-settlement New England had low numbers of wildlife that depended on grassland habitats, but these species increased as early settlers cleared the land for farming. The reduction in farming activity over the past 150 years, and the reliance on the limited remaining agricultural land, made many wildlife species increasingly vulnerable. Although early mowing of hay and sediment run-off from farms can be detrimental to some wildlife, agriculture provides a net benefit by sustaining valuable habitat for wild animals (Oehler, 2005). The NH Fish and Game Department's Comprehensive Wildlife Conservation Plan identified large grassland parcels of greater than 10 acres as important features for associated wildlife. Most larger grassland acreage occurs in Grafton County, followed by Merrimack and Coos Counties (Oehler, 2005). These areas have the most dairy farms in the state.

A nationwide survey of farmers showed that 80 percent of the respondents had experienced wildlife damage to their crops and 53 percent indicated that the dependence exceeded their tolerance. This type of wildlife damge is an indication that agricultural fields maintained by farmers provide feed for many wild animals (Drake, D., and Grand, J., 2002).

Wildlife Species

Field acreage is especially important for a small group of bird species that require grasslands as their primary habitat. In New Hampshire the main species of concern are bobolink, Eastern meadowlark, grasshopper sparrow, savannah sparrow, vesper sparrow, and upland sandpiper. These six grassland bird species all nest on the ground and they feed primarily on insects and weed seeds found immediately within fields. These birds are considered "area sensitive" in that they don't occur in fields smaller than a minimum critical acreage. On the low end of the scale are bobolinks, which typically don't occur in fields less than five acres in size; Eastern meadowlarks require fields larger than 15 acres; savannah sparrows require fields larger than 20 acres; and grasshopper sparrows and vesper sparrows require fields larger than 30 acres. On the upper end of the scale are upland sandpipers that require fields at least 100 acres in size. Because all these birds nest directly on the ground, their eggs and young are especially vulnerable to predation from coyotes, foxes, skunks, and raccoons – predators that tend to concentrate their hunting activities on field edges. The specific minimum field acreage required by grassland birds is likely determined by their attempt to avoid predation, as well as the specific territory size of each bird species.

Meadowlark - Victor Young artwork

As the availability of large-acreage fields declines in New Hampshire, so do the wildlife species requiring these fields. In her book "History of New Hampshire Game and Furbearers," author Hellenette Silver reports that by the 1880s, (the peak of agriculture in the state), nearly every field in the Merrimack River Valley had one or more nesting pairs of upland sandpipers; today, there is only a single breeding population of this species in New Hampshire, located at the Pease International Tradeport in Newington.

Currently, upland sandpipers and grasshopper sparrows are listed as state-endangered and state-threatened species, respectively, and their numbers continue to decline as the result of habitat loss due to development, changing field management practices, and reversion of fields to forest. These factors have resulted in the extirpation of at least one grassland bird species from the state in recent history - the Henslow's sparrow, a bird of weedy old fields whose closest breeding population is now in western New York State.

Bobolink - Victor Young artwork

Habitat

Structure, or how a field "looks" is a primary factor in determining what wildlife species will use a given field and for what purpose. Most wildlife species base their main habitat choices on structure, and then refine their selection based on other factors, such as what plant species are present. The average height and density of plants within a field determines the field's habitat structure and its suitability for each wildlife species.

Tall (higher than two feet), dense grasses which are often associated with high-production hayfields provide ideal nesting and feeding opportunities for grassland birds such as bobolinks and Eastern meadowlarks, and cover for wild turkeys and white-tailed deer. Some wildlife species, such as killdeer, horned larks and chipping sparrows, prefer short-grass habitats like those found in closely-grazed pastures or on soils with poor fertility; these species nest on the ground in shallow depressions and feed primarily on weed seeds and insects they find within short-grasses.

However, the majority of wildlife species associated with agricultural fields prefer habitats that contain a mixture of tall grass and short grass areas; such a situation may occur with two adjacent fields that have different mowing regimes (e.g., hayfield and adjacent pasture), fields managed through rotational grazing, or managed hayfields that contain wet areas mowed only late in the season. Such situations provide a diversity of cover and feeding opportunities in close proximity to one another and allow wildlife to meet a variety of their habitat needs.

Canada Geese - Victor Young artwork

The timing and frequency of field mowing or grazing are two of the most important factors that determine if and how a specific wildlife species will use a field. Most obviously, mowing/grazing immediately affect plant height and density, which determines the structure provided to wildlife within the field. Additionally, how frequently the field is mowed/grazed (e.g., multiple cuttings per year, once yearly, once every other year or less frequently) can directly influence plant species composition and nutritional quality of forages within the field. Generally, as mowing frequency decreases, the diversity of plant species within a field increases, as does the number of wildlife species that will use the field.

Fields mowed two or more times each year tend to be dominated by only a few plant species, often a couple of cool-season legumes (e.g., red or white clover, alfalfa, vetch) and a couple of grasses (e.g., timothy, orchard grass, Kentucky bluegrass). Farmers employ frequent mowing to harvest forage crops when they are at their highest nutritional value, to stimulate additional growth of high-quality forage, and to discourage "weed" species from invading the fields. This frequent mowing can also produce a high-protein, highly-digestible food source for wildlife species such as deer, black bear, woodchuck, cottontail rabbit, porcupine, wild turkey and Canada goose.

Cool-season legume-grass fields are especially important to deer and bears in early spring, a time when these animals are recovering from the stresses of winter and when few other forages are available. Deer continue to forage in such fields regularly through late-spring, when high-quality food is especially important for supporting lactation in does and early antler development in bucks. Wild turkeys will graze on young leaves and buds of legumes and grasses, but more importantly, they are attracted to fields to feed on insects; frequent mowing often stimulates dense re-sprouting of legumes, creating ideal habitat for crickets and grasshoppers which are an important source of protein for adult turkeys and growing turkey poults.

Modern farming practices that harvest several cuttings of grass per season may be detrimental to some species, but beneficial to many others and help maintain open space that would otherwise be taken over by development. Hunters, snowmobilers and others use this land for outdoor recreation.

Wild Turkeys

Wild turkeys are a great success story of a bird that has been restored to agricultural habitats in New Hampshire. Wild turkey restoration efforts in New Hampshire date back to the 1960s. A dramatic increase in the turkey population has occurred since the transplant of 25 New York turkeys to New Hampshire in 1975. Now the population is estimated at more than 25,000 birds, making this a very successful wildlife project. Wild turkeys have the potential to become a major game species in New Hampshire in terms of man-hours of recreation. During the 2003 season there were 16,000 permit holders for turkey hunting (Walski, 2005, pp. 9, 12). These hunters not only help fill local coffers with their hunting license revenue, but they also purchase gas, lodging and hunting supplies that boost the economy.

The farming activities associated with dairying are favorable for the establishment of a wild turkey population. Ted Walski of the NH Fish and Game Department stated that, "Dairy farms are synonymous with large turkey flocks, because the corn wastage in manure spreading and manure piles, and corn silage in the bunker and pit silos have provided winter food and the fields associated with farmland have provided the best summer turkey brood habitat" (Walksi, 2005, p. 31). Dairy farming plays a key role in maintaining wild turkeys and attracting the hunters.

Field demonstration of grain threshing circa 1930s - 1940s.

Dairy farming also helps support many businesses related to the production of milk, such as feed stores, milking equipment suppliers, and tractor dealerships. These industries are part of the infrastructure needed to provide fresh milk to consumers. These auxiliary industries create jobs and use material goods which benefit the state's economy. Shown above is Blackmount Equipment, Inc., North Haverhill, NH.

Economic Model

The Impact of Cattle Farming on the New Hampshire Economy

Abstract

The impact of cattle farming on the New Hampshire economy was investigated using the economic impact model software IMPLAN Plus®. The cattle farming industry numbers in the IMPLAN database included dairy cows, heifer replacements, calves, dairy goats and beef. The cash receipts for milk, beef, calves, field corn and hay sales were used to estimate the level of economic activity of cattle farming and were taken from the 2002 Annual Statistical Bulletin published by New England Agricultural Statistics Service (NASS). The dairy farm cash receipts comprised more than 75 percent of total cash receipts for the farming industry.

The results indicate that cattle farming impacts the state and local economies with more than $141 million in total output, 3,717 jobs, and more than $19 million in labor income. In addition, the industry provides over $7 million in state and local government tax receipts.

The economic multipliers summarize the cumulative effects of an initial change in final demand plus spending in the local economy. The output and labor multipliers of 1.84 and 4.03, respectively, suggest that for each dollar produced, the cattle industry generates an additional $0.84 in output and $3.03 in labor income. Most of the impact is in the indirect effects: $0.70 and $2.23 per $1 output and labor income, respectively. The employment multiplier of 1.52 suggests that with each $1 million change in output, the cattle farming industry adds an additional 0.52 jobs to the state economy.

Introduction

In the past, impact studies of open space, lakes, rivers and ponds, and agriculture on the New Hampshire state economy were conducted. For example, the Resource System Group estimated the impact of open space on the state's economy. In 1997, the impact of agricultural activities, not including greenhouse production, ornamental horticulture, landscaping and food processing, were determined to have annual gross revenues of $413 million. Of these revenues, 56 percent were dependent upon open space. Open space was defined as areas that are not built up, excavated or developed. These included wild areas, forests, tree farms, open productive agricultural land, grassland, pastures, wetlands, lakes and natural seashores. Out of $413 million, the total direct and indirect effects from agriculture were $377 million and 5,400 jobs, and almost $31 million in state and local tax revenues (Resource System Group, 1999).

The Institute for New Hampshire Studies reported $605 million in total agriculture sales plus $125 million in dairy and specialty food products in fiscal year 2002. It was estimated that of the total $605 million, $310 million was derived from farm sales that included direct sales, sales to manufacturers and sales to other farmers (Goss, 2003). The $310 million sales resulted in an additional $415 million to the state economy, 2,414 full-time jobs, $70 million in household income and $15.6 million in tax receipts (Goss, 2003).

Because farmland is important in supplying land for recreation and protection of aquifers, another study that addressed the economic values from recreational uses of fishing, swimming, boating and public drinking water supply was reviewed (Shapiro and Kroll, 2003). The annual sales generated by recreational uses of New Hampshire's freshwaters ranged from $1.1 billion to as much as $1.5 billion annually.

To date, no study has been conducted in New Hampshire to document the impact of cattle farming, both dollar value of output and labor income and number of jobs on the state and local economies. The purpose of this study is to estimate the direct, indirect, and induced impacts of cattle farming on the New Hampshire economy and to determine the top five industries that are affected by cattle farming.

Materials and Methods

To estimate the total value of production, cash receipts reported by the 2002 NASS-NE Bulletin were used as indicators of the cattle farming industry's economic activity. The total cash receipts from sales of cattle, beef, milk, hay and field crops were $76,909,700 in 2001 ($51,248,000 milk; $6,356,700 cattle from dairies; $7,063,000 from beef; $3,716,000 hay; $8,526,000 field corn). The milk and cattle sales from dairy farms comprise 75 percent of the total receipts for the cattle industry.

The cattle farming industry consists of businesses producing goods and services. The goods are milk, calves for sale, beef, field corn and hay. Services include any service performed by a farm for pay, but these services are not independent custom service businesses.

In 2001, there were a total of 900 cattle operations. These operations included 171 state-licensed commercial dairies, plus heifer replacement operations, beef cattle and calf production operations. It also included farms with at least one beef or dairy cow on hand during a year. The total of milk cows in the state was 18,000, but the total number of dairy cattle was higher if replacement heifers were taken into account. The Dairy Herd Improvement Association (the dairy herd management record system) records show an average 28 percent culling rate per herd. This would translate into 10,080 replacements, so the total number of dairy cattle would be around 28,000 to 29,000. The average milk production per cow per year was 17,944 lbs (U.S. Census of Agriculture, 2002). The data set did not distinguish as to whether the heifer replacement operations were part of the dairy farms or independent businesses. By the nature of New Hampshire dairy farms, it can be assumed that most heifer raising was part of the dairy operation; thus, the cash receipts and the economic impact from these operations are included in the dairy farm cash receipts.

Input-output analysis using the Minnesota Implan Group (MIG) modeling software IMPLAN Pro® was used to analyze the impact of farming on the New Hampshire economy and to derive the economic multipliers. The database provided by MIG contained 509 different sectors in all 10 counties in New Hampshire. This information was then used to develop an input-output model for the study area.

The cattle farming industry was selected to model the impact of dairy farms on the state economy. Although dairy farming is classified as a single industry in the North American Industry Classification System database (NCAIS), it is not an independent industry in the MIG database. The MIG database combines dairy, heifer replacement, calf, beef and milking goat operations into a single industry.

The total cash receipt value from sales was used as an input level to calculate multipliers that estimate the economic contribution of the industry being analyzed on total output, employment, and labor income. The direct, indirect and induced impacts for sectors are measured in millions of dollars. Results for output and labor income effects are in 2001 dollars. Impact of employment is measured in total jobs, both full time and part time. The resulting multipliers are measures of a change. The output and labor income multipliers measure direct, indirect, and induced change per dollar of change in the industry's output. The employment multipliers measure direct, indirect and induced employment effects from the production of an additional $1 million of output.

The direct effects are changes in the industries to which a final demand change was made. It is the response for a given industry per $1 million of final demand for that same industry. The final demand is then defined as goods and services purchased for their ultimate use by an end user. These goods and services are not used in any process of production; they disappear from the economy. The direct output is consumed within the industry. Direct effects are changes in the industry used to describe the event being analyzed.

The indirect effects are the changes in purchases in industries related to, or supporting cattle farming as they respond to the new demands. The related industries are feed mills, equipment dealers, veterinary services, etc. These effects represent the responses resulting from purchasing and repurchasing among industries per $1 million of final demand for cattle farming. It is the result of the interaction between cattle farming and supplier businesses.

The induced effects reflect changes in spending from households to purchase the products of the cattle farming industry as income increases or decreases due to the changes in production. It represents the response by all local industries caused by the expenditures of new household income generated by the direct and indirect effects per $1 million of final demand of the cattle industry.

Results and Discussion

Table 1 summarizes the annual economic impact of cattle farming on the state's economy. It is the dollar contribution of dairy farms plus cattle operations related to dairy, heifer replacement, dairy beef and beef operations to the state economy.

Table 1. Output, employment and labor income for cattle farming.

	Output 2001 Dollars	Employment Number of Jobs	Labor Income 2001 Dollars
Direct	$76,909,700	2,444.6	$4,826,707
Indirect	$54,232,430	1,148.1	$10,805,118
Induced	$10,853,286	124.9	$3,831,419
Total Impact	$141,995,696	3,717.5	$19,463,244

The direct impact of almost $77 million represents the cash receipts received by dairy, beef and dairy goat farmers for their products. An additional $65 million was added to the state's economy from the original $77 million in sales by the cattle farming sector. The indirect impact was $54.2 million, which is the dollar value cattle farms generate by interacting with local suppliers. For example, purchasing milking equipment, tractor parts or feed from a local dealer is included in this impact. The induced impact is $10.8 million. This is the money that consumers spend to purchase cattle and dairy farm products such as milk, ice cream, yogurt, cheese or beef in grocery stores or restaurants.

The cattle farming industry also contributed an additional 3,717 jobs to the state economy, $19.4 million in labor income and over $7 million in state and local government tax receipts that include property taxes, personal taxes, licenses and fees. Of the 3,717 jobs that produced taxable income, 2,444 jobs remained within the cattle industry, 1,148 jobs were created by industries related to farming and 125 jobs were created in restaurants, grocery stores, hospitals, etc. due to changes in household spending that resulted from the industry's economic activity in the state.

In 2001, there were 18,000 cows producing milk in New Hampshire, and dairy farms contributed 75 percent of the farm receipts from all cattle, dairy sheep, and goat farms. The total impact would then be $5,926 per cow, that is $3,204 in direct, $2,259 in indirect, and $452 in induced effects per dairy cow. Additionally, one cow would impact labor income by $810.

The vast majority of New Hampshire farmers purchase most of their inputs locally, and the loss of these farms would have an impact on other local businesses as well. For example, with each $1 million less output from the cattle sector, the indirect output effect would decrease by more than $700,000, and indirect labor income would decrease by $140,000. The total loss would be $1.7 million. Additionally, the local farm-supporting businesses would lose 15 jobs. The sectors that would suffer most from losing cattle farms are hay-producing farms; businesses that provide services that are an essential part of agricultural production, such as land clearing, water supply, and custom harvest; and wholesale trade, local power suppliers, veterinary services, truck transportation and insurance carriers.

In addition, due to the $1 million less in the local economy, an induced effect would be smaller as well. Almost two jobs will be lost within the local economy. Industries that would be affected by the lower farming output are expenditures that are paid to run a farmstead, primarily utilities, property taxes, etc., and all businesses involved with these commodities. Hospitals, restaurants, wholesale trade, motor vehicle and parts dealers, and insurance carriers will be affected as well.

However, it is necessary to realize that the estimated economic losses presented here are directly connected to the dollar value of the cattle or dairy farm production. In 2001, cattle farms were farming a total of 135,583 acres of land (U.S. Census of New Hampshire Agriculture, 2002). This acreage is an important part of the 5.2 million acres of open space in the state, because it also serves as hunting grounds and snowmobile trails and for other recreational outdoor activities.

Table 2 shows the output, employment, and labor income multipliers for the cattle farming industry.

Table 2. Output, employment and labor income multipliers.

	Output[1]	Labor Income[1]
Direct	1.00	1.00
Indirect	0.70	2.23
Induced	0.14	0.80
Total Impact	1.84	4.03

1) Output and Labor income multipliers are for changes in dollars per dollar change in the cattle farming industry.

The total output multiplier indicates how many dollars' worth of indirect and induced effects are generated for each additional dollar produced by the cattle farming sector. For example, for each additional dollar produced by the cattle farming industry, $0.70 worth of indirect output is generated by other industries. These industries are local businesses supplying farms with feed, milking equipment, machinery, auto parts, construction, and other crop-producing supplies, and services including engineering, veterinary, power-generating, insurance, wholesalers and warehouses. An additional $0.14 worth of induced output is generated by increased household spending due to the cattle farming activities. The induced impact includes restaurants, health clinics and hospitals, food and beverage stores, real estate and legal services, and telecommunications. In total, the cattle industry generates an additional $0.84 for each dollar produced.

The output multipliers can be used to gauge the interdependence of sectors. The larger the output multiplier, the greater the interdependence of the sector or industry on the rest of the local economy. The multiplier 1.84 would suggest a high interdependence on the local economy. This could be affected by the fact that this industry purchases nearly all inputs locally.

According to the MIG model, the regional purchase coefficient (the percentage of all inputs spent locally for this industry) of 0.65 indicates that local industries provide approximately 65 percent of commodity supplies for the cattle industry. The remaining 35 percent, which represents a value of approximately $30 million, is imported from other states. This difference would suggest that there is an opportunity for dairy or beef farm supporting businesses to work with New Hampshire producers. It can be assumed that dairy farms have a large share in this impact, as they contribute a large portion to the total sales. Milk, cattle and calf sales from dairy farms comprise more than 75 percent of all cash receipts in this industry.

The labor income multipliers show the direct, indirect and induced labor income for both employee compensation and proprietor income generated per dollar of output. The indirect effect multiplier would suggest that the farm supply businesses benefit most from cattle farming, as they receive $2.23 in labor income per $1 of income in the cattle industry. The induced effect is an additional $.80 per $1 income in the industry. For example, if a dairy farm hires a herdsman and he or she increases the operation's output by $20,000, the total impact would be over $80,000 in total labor income in the state economy.

Table 3 depicts changes in employment due to changes in output in the industry. These changes are measured in number of jobs, both full time and part time, per $1 million change in output. For example, with each $1 million dollar output increase, 48 jobs would be created.

Table 3. Employment multiplier for cattle farming.

	Employment Effect[1]	Multipliers[2]
Direct	32.78	1.00
Indirect	14.92	0.46
Induced	1.62	0.06
Total Impact	48.33	1.52

[1]) Employment effect is number of jobs change per $1 million changes in output.

[2]) Employment multipliers are changes in jobs per one job in cattle farming.

Fifteen jobs in supporting businesses or industries and 1.62 jobs in induced effects or other businesses are generated for $1 million in output change. In other words, one additional job in cattle farming creates 0.52 additional jobs in the state, with the majority in farm-supporting businesses.

The difference between Table 1 and Table 3 in employment effects is that in Table 1, the employment effects represent jobs in the state and local economies generated by cattle farming at a specific income level, while Table 3 shows changes in jobs being generated by $1 million output increase.

Conclusion

The revenue from agriculture sales, specifically dairy and beef farms, may seem negligible compared to revenues from sales generated by the state's leading industry-tourism. However, it is important to realize that productive agricultural land is part of the open space we value. In 2001, cattle farmers were farming 135,583 acres of crop land and managing a total of 206,000 acres of land, which is an important part of the 5.2 million acres of open space.

The revenue of $310 million from agricultural sales constituted only 0.7 percent of the estimated gross state product for New Hampshire for fiscal year 2002, and the sales from cattle farms represent a smaller portion of the gross state product in 2001, 0.17 percent.

The cattle farming industry impacts the state economy with more than $141 million, which is an average of $157,700 per cattle operation and over $5,900 per milking cow. After excluding the 202 farms with one to nine beef or dairy cows (U.S. Census of Agriculture, 2002), the average economic impact per farm increases to almost $203,000. It was also determined that one dairy cow would impact labor income by $810.

For related cattle farming businesses using an additional worker or, in some cases, sustain themselves, a cattle farm must produce approximately $70,000 in output, or almost $1 million to sustain a worker in grocery stores or restaurants.

Making loose hay with horse and wagon,

circa 1930s to 1940s.

The Cost of Producing Milk on New Hampshire Dairy Farms

Farm records provide the best means of measuring financial performance and determining the cost of producing milk on commercial dairy farms. Unfortunately, since the 1980s, there have been no published, financial record summaries available for New Hampshire dairy farms. The next best source of farm level data appears in the annual Northeast Dairy Farm Summary prepared by the Northeast Farm Credit Services. (Northeast Farm Credit Services include Farm Credit of Maine, Farm Credit of Western New York, First Pioneer Farm Credit and Yankee Farm Credit.) These annual summaries report detailed financial and production information for commercial dairies located across New England.

In recent years, data from more than 130 New England dairy farms have appeared in the annual Northeast Dairy Farm Summary. Although this is only a fraction of dairy farms located in New England, the numbers are sufficient to provide a reasonable starting point for estimating financial performance on New Hampshire farms.

Before using this information, it is important to recognize the farms included in the Northeast Dairy Farm Summary represent progressive, above-average dairy operations. In fact, average cows per farm and milk production per cow are higher than the typical New England dairy.

More representative estimates of cow numbers per farm and milk production per cow for New Hampshire are reported in the Annual Statistical Bulletin published by the New England Agricultural Statistics Service. (See www.nass.usda.gov/Statistics_by_State/New_England/.)

New Hampshire Dairy Farm Profile

What does the financial picture look like on New Hampshire dairy farms in recent years? Before examining the cost of producing milk, it may be useful to understand the nature of receipts and expenses on a typical New Hampshire dairy farm. Averaging several years of information provides a long-term profile of a farm's financial health. Table 1 shows a financial profile for a New Hampshire dairy farm. This profile was developed using 2000 through 2006 New England farm data reported in the Northeast Dairy Farm Summaries adjusted for average New Hampshire farm size, milk production levels, and milk prices. Cows per farm, milk production and milk price were based on New Hampshire data reported by the New England Agricultural Statistical Service.

The average herd size for the New Hampshire profile is 110 dairy cows. With total farm receipts at $363,350 and farm expenses at $336,530, annual net income averaged $26,820 per farm. Since the typical New Hampshire dairy is an owner-operator family farm, net income is the dollar amount available to cover the owner's labor and management costs, any unpaid family labor, and a charge for owner's equity.

Malnati Farm - Walpole, NH.

Table 1. New Hampshire Dairy Farm Profile.

Units	Per Farm	Per Cow	Per Hundredweight of Milk Sold
Average number of cows	110	---	---
Pounds of milk sold	2,035,000	18,500	---
Crop acres	274	2.5	---
Worker equivalents	2.76	---	---
Receipts, Expenses and Net Income			
Milk sales	$ 303,670	$ 2,761	$ 14.92
Cattle sales	18,860	171	0.93
Crop sales	8,860	81	0.44
Other	31,960	290	1.57
Total receipts	$ 363,350	$ 3,303	$ 17.85
Chemicals & sprays	$ 2,190	$ 20	$ 0.11
Custom hire	11,830	108	0.58
Depreciation	26,340	239	1.29
Feed purchased	92,210	838	4.53
Fertilizer & lime	10,860	99	0.53
Freight & trucking	16,020	146	0.79
Gasoline, fuel & oil	12,040	109	0.59
Insurance	6,600	60	0.32
Interest paid	16,590	151	0.82
Labor hired	42,070	382	2.07
Rent	7,180	65	0.35
Repairs	22,610	206	1.11
Seeds & plants	4,500	41	0.22
Supplies	23,990	218	1.18
Taxes	5,760	52	0.28
Utilities	8,310	76	0.41
Veterinary & medicine	15,070	137	0.74
Other	12,360	112	0.61
Total expenses	$ 336,530	$ 3,059	$ 16.53
Net farm income	$ 26,820	$ 244	$ 1.32
Family living expenses & income taxes paid	$ 32,180	$ 293	$ 1.58
Assets, Liabilities and Equity			
Total farm asset value	$ 996,410	$ 9,058	---
Total farm liabilities	303,240	2,757	---
Owner's equity	$ 693,170	$6,302	---

Milk sales were 84 percent of total farm receipts. The amount of milk sold per cow averaged 18,500 pounds (2,151 gallons) with milk receipts per cow at $2,761. This resulted in an average milk price of $14.92 per hundredweight ($1.74 per gallon). Farm receipts also included cattle sales, crop sales and other non-milk items. Other non-milk items consist of service and product sales from secondary enterprises such as maple syrup, cordwood, compost, custom work and agri-tourism, and may include government program payments. Combining all farm sales, total farm receipts rose to $3,303 per cow or $17.85 per hundredweight.

Farm expenses equaled $3,059 per cow or $16.53 per hundredweight of milk before taking into account the value of unpaid labor and management, and a charge for owner's equity. Purchased feed and hired labor costs were the two largest expenses equaling 40 percent of the total. Other top expenses were depreciation, supplies, repairs, interest, freight and trucking, and veterinary and medicine costs. If combined, crop production costs (fertilizer and lime, seeds and plant, and chemical and sprays) would be listed among the top farm expenses.

The net farm income of $26,820 equaled $244 per cow or $1.32 per hundredweight. Based on the information provided by farmers in the Northeast Dairy Farm Summary, average family living expenses and income taxes paid by this size operation were $32,180. Family living expenses and income taxes paid were $5,360 greater than net farm income.

Estimated total farm asset value for a typical New Hampshire dairy farm was $996,410 with total farm liabilities of $303,240. Owner's equity was $693,170 or $6,302 per cow. Seventy percent of the farm's value was owned by the farm family clear and free of debt. Given the source of the farm data, this estimate is more than likely higher than the average New Hampshire dairy farm. Dairy farms with higher levels of debt would have less equity and a larger interest expense.

Cost of Producing Milk in New Hampshire

The cost of producing milk is determined by dividing farm expenses by the quantity of milk sold. The calculation is simple; however, difficulties arise in identifying all appropriate costs and dealing with the costs of producing livestock, crops and other items which give rise to farm receipts.

Calculations for the cost of producing milk on New Hampshire dairy farms from 2000 to 2006 are shown in Table 2. As with the profile in Table 1, these estimates are based on the 2000 through 2006 New England farm data reported in the Northeast Dairy Farm Summaries adjusted for average New Hampshire farm size and milk production levels.

Farm expenses are often classified as either a variable or fixed expense. Variable expenses are those costs which are directly related to immediate or short-term changes in production, such as purchasing additional grain to increase milk sales or hiring additional help when cows are added. In the short-run, variable costs can be eliminated by ceasing production. Variable expenses per farm were $238,700 in 2000, reaching a high of $310,010 in 2006. Over the seven-year period, total variable farm expenses rose 30 percent. Much of this increase was due to greater number of cows per farm and more milk sold per cow.

Table 2. Cost of Producing Milk, New Hampshire Dairy Farms.

Year	2000	2001	2002	2003	2004	2005	2006
Cows per farm	108	105	106	113	114	114	115
Milk sold, pounds	1,871,960	1,878,350	1,931,530	2,154,120	2,158,930	2,151,750	2,246,300
Variable farm expenses	$ 238,700	$ 251,840	$ 246,610	$ 266,940	$ 301,830	$ 299,460	$ 310,010
Plus: Fixed farm expenses	68,150	66,680	62,360	62,580	69,370	70,420	68,730
Plus: Value of unpaid labor & management	63,120	60,220	64,780	77,570	73,560	73,380	73,820
Plus: Interest on equity capital (5%)	31,460	31,030	32,080	33,760	36,700	40,340	40,650
Minus: Cattle sales, crop sales & other non-milk receipts	62,910	46,630	65,710	63,010	63,910	57,450	59,950
Equals: Cost of milk production per farm	$ 338,520	$ 363,140	$ 340,120	$ 377,840	$ 417,550	$ 426,150	$ 433,260
Divided by: Hundredweight of milk sold	18,720	18,784	19,315	21,541	21,589	21,518	22,463
Equals: Cost of producing milk per hundredweight	$ 18.08	$ 19.33	$ 17.61	$ 17.54	$ 19.34	$ 19.80	$ 19.29
Per gallon cost of producing milk	$ 2.10	$ 2.25	$ 2.05	$ 2.04	$ 2.25	$ 2.30	$ 2.24

Fixed expenses are those costs related to the size of the business and are closely associated with investments in machinery, cattle, buildings and land. Fixed farm expenses shown in Table 2 include depreciation, insurance, most of the interest expense, half of the repair costs, taxes and the portion of other expenses related to cow replacement. In the short run, fixed costs do not change regardless of production level. Depreciation on a building will still occur regardless of the number of cows milked. Property taxes have to be paid even if there are no farm receipts. Fixed expenses per farm ranged from a low of $62,360 in 2002 to a high of $70,420 in 2005.

Since the New England dairy farm data from the Northeast Dairy Farm Summaries represent financial information for farms operated as single-family proprietorships, expenses do not include charges for the owner's labor and management, unpaid family labor, and owner's equity. Estimates of these missing expenses are needed to get an accurate calculation of the cost of producing milk.

The owner's labor and management costs equal what the owner (farmer) could earn as a hired manager for a dairy operation of similar size or as a manager of a firm in a position with similar responsibilities. Unpaid family labor costs may simply be estimated as additional wages paid for similar work done on the farm. Neither of these cost estimates is collected for the New England dairy farm data. (An alternative approach would be to use what the farm owner identifies as family living expenses and income taxes paid. This approach often results in a conservative estimate of the cost of producing milk.)

Relying on USDA milk production costs for the Northern Crescent region of the United States, charges for operator labor and management and unpaid family labor can be approximated. Adjusting for differences in farm size and accounting for hired labor costs, annual estimates for the value of unpaid labor and management on New Hampshire farms ranged from $60,220 to $77,570 over the seven-year period. (USDA Northern Crescent data for 2000 to 2005 may be found at http://www.ers.usda.gov/Data/CostsAndReturns/. Since 2006 data is not yet available, 2005 estimates were used for 2006. These USDA labor costs were first adjusted downward to reflect efficiencies associated with larger New Hampshire farm size compared to the Northern Crescent data. Then New Hampshire hired labor costs were subtracted from the sum of USDA hired labor costs and USDA opportunity cost of unpaid labor to get an estimate for the value of unpaid labor and management on New Hampshire farms.)

A charge for owner's equity is determined using the rate of return which could be earned by the farmer's money invested in the dairy had the farmer invested the money elsewhere. This charge recognizes that there is a cost associated with tying up money over many years in a business.

Historically, traditional farms earn rates of return on equity from 4 to 6 percent. There are many reasons why farmers are willing to accept this low rate of return. Among them are personal satisfaction associated with the farming way of life and anticipation of long-term gains in the value of real property. For the purpose of determining the cost of producing milk on New Hampshire farms, a five percent rate of return was applied against the farmer's equity.

When determining the cost of producing milk, the issue of non-milk receipts does not pose a significant problem for the typical New Hampshire dairy farm since non-milk receipts are seldom more than 10 to 20 percent of total farm receipts. Therefore, total farm expenses may be credited for non-milk sales by adjusting expenses downward by an equivalent dollar value. This calculation assumes that non-milk products incur expenses equivalent to their receipts.

Following through the above calculations, the cost of producing milk on New Hampshire dairy farms was $338,520 per farm in 2000, climbing to $433,260 per farm in 2006. Dividing the cost of producing milk by the corresponding amount of milk sold results in costs of producing milk, which range from $17.54 to $19.80 per hundredweight ($2.04 to $2.30 per gallon).

Cost of Production versus Price Received

How do the costs of producing milk compare with the actual prices received? Figure 1 shows average annual milk price reported by New England Agricultural Statistical Service (NASS) compared to the cost of milk production for New Hampshire dairy farms over the past seven years. Over the entire period, farmers have been selling milk at less than their production costs.

Figure 1. Milk Price vs. Cost of Milk Production, New Hampshire Dairy Farms.

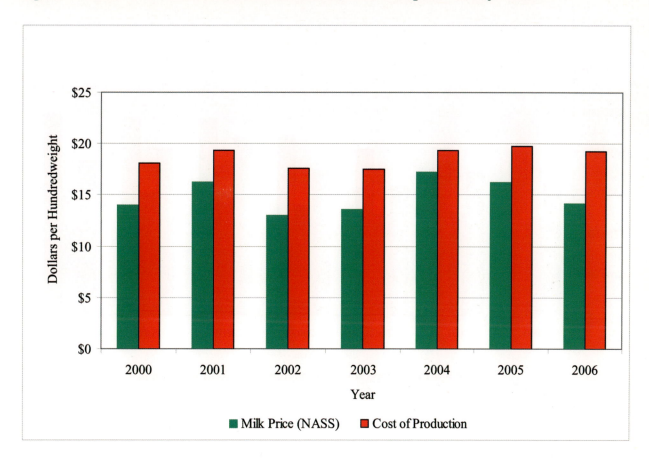

Converting the milk price received per hundredweight to gallons, the prices farmers received for milk ranged from $1.51 to $2.01 per gallon during the 2000 to 2007 period; whereas, the cost of producing a gallon of milk averaged from $2.04 to $2.30 over the same period. (See Table 2.)

How can dairy farmers continue to produce milk if they don't cover their costs of production? The reason lies partly with the nature of the expenses incurred. Earlier, farm expenses were classified as variable and fixed. Over a short-run period such as a year, variable expenses fall under the "farmer's control", i.e. they can be eliminated by stopping production. On the other hand, in the same period of time the farm operation will incur fixed costs, regardless of the amount of production. As long as a farmer is able to generate receipts greater than variable costs, it is a wise economic decision to produce milk in that short-run period because the receipts in excess of variable costs will defray the fixed expenses.

Figure 2 compares total receipts to variable farm expenses and to total farm expenses for New Hampshire dairy farms from 2000 through 2006. The receipt bar appears first for each year and includes milk sales and other farm receipts. The variable expense bar follows the receipt bar, while the total expense bar is last. Total expenses include variable expenses, fixed expenses, value of unpaid labor and management, and charge on owner's equity.

Figure 2. Farm Receipts vs. Farm Expenses, New Hampshire Dairy Farms.

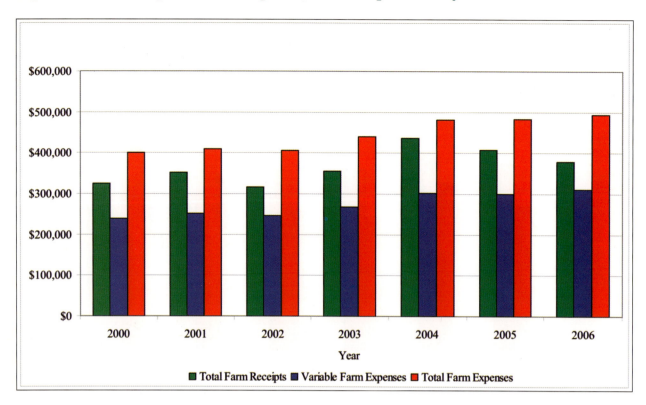

Although dairy farmers weren't able to cover their total expenses in any year, they did have receipts in excess of variable costs. New Hampshire dairy farmers came closest to covering all costs in 2004.

The obvious conclusion is that this situation is not sustainable. If it exists for many years, farms start to show signs of deterioration and farm families become stressed as they are unable to make sufficient income to cover family living expenses. In the long-run, dairy farmers exit the industry and seek employment elsewhere. The land and farm property are sold and often become used for other ventures.

From 2000 to 2006, the number of commercial dairy operations in New England reported by NASS decreased from 2,701 to 2,025, a drop of 25 percent. Commercial dairy operations in New Hampshire went from 176 to 130, a 26 percent decrease over the same time period.

Field crop meeting for farmers, circa 1930s - 1940s.

Fairchild Dairy Teaching and Research Center, Durham, NH.

The University of New Hampshire and the State's Dairy Industry

The University of New Hampshire has a long, well-established relationship with the New Hampshire and New England dairy industry. In 1887 the New Hampshire Agricultural Experiment Station began as a department in the New Hampshire College of Agriculture and Mechanic Arts. The first director of the station was G.H. Whitcher, professor of Agriculture (Collins, 1987). The experiment station began as two departments (Dairy, Field and Feeding). A.H.W. Wood was superintendent of the Dairy Department and Whitcher was in charge of Field and Feeding (Collins, 1987). So began the commitment of the University to the state's dairy industry. Early bulletins from the station discussed silage, fertilization, feeding studies and manure applications. It is interesting that much of the research conducted by the dairy researchers today cover the same categories.

Dairy Cattle Research

The University of New Hampshire has a long and hallowed history in regards to its contribution to the dairy industry. Dr. E. G. Ritzman conducted research involving metabolism of ruminants.

A respiration chamber (calorimeter) was designed by F.G. Benedict, director of the Nutrition Laboratory, for research with large domestic animals. This equipment allowed for determination of carbon dioxide production of animals as an indicator of metabolism (Collins, 1987). This equipment was subsequently used by many researchers to help determine the energy requirements of livestock, including dairy cattle, and is the foundation for the energy values used in dairy cattle nutrition today. Ritzman and N.F. Colovos designed an apparatus for automatic collection of solid and liquid excreta from cows to aid in the determination of digestibility of feedstuffs (Collins, 1987).

K.S. Morrow conducted calf research to investigate how calves perform on a powdered skim milk formula and weaning at 7 weeks of age. This was some of the earliest calf milk replacer research conducted (Collins, 1987). Research studying the nutrition of preweaned and postweaned calves continues at UNH today. In the 1940s, H.A. Keener, G.P Percival, and Morrow determined that a deficiency of cobalt afflicted many cattle in Carroll County and feeding cobalt sulphate quickly corrected the deficiency. Feed manufacturers now add cobalt to dairy diets, thus inhibiting cobalt deficiency. Keener, Percival, Colovos, Morrow and agricultural chemist, A. E. Teeri also studied vitamins A and D as they related to calf nutrition and the use of sulfur dioxide as a silage preservative (Collins, 1987).

Bacteriologist L.W. Slanetz, along with F.E. Allen and Morrow studied mastitis and isolated several hundred bacterial strains. Keener and H.C. Moore studied grass silage harvesting and storage and recommended practices to avoid foul smelling and butyric acid containing material. Keener also explained the Vitamin D content of silage, resulting in the suggestion that first cut be made into silage and the second cut be made into hay. In the 1960s, and 1970s, dairy cattle research focused on urea inclusion to lactating cow diets, the digestibility of various ration components and the metabolism of various minerals especially copper. In the 1970s, dairy researcher C.G. Schwab joined J.B. Holter. Research emphasis included the determination of dry matter intake equations for dairy cattle. These equations are the foundation for the equations used by feed companies today. Schwab's research with calves determined that the amino acid methionine is first limiting for calf growth. Holter also studied the effect of different ratios of forage components as they relate to lactating cow performance. He also developed one of the earliest programmable ration balancing programs used in the dairy industry.

In the 1990s, research conducted at UNH helped dairy producers understand how fat supplementation can improve milk production. Through the 1980s and continuing today, Schwab has made the University of New Hampshire world-renowned in the area of protein nutrition of the dairy cow. Through his research, we now know that methionine and lysine are the two limiting amino acids in the diet of cows for milk protein synthesis. His research is used globally by dairy producers to correctly balance protein fractions for calves to lactating cows resulting in reduced feed costs to producers and lowering N emissions. In the late 1990s, P.S. Erickson joined the department with a research emphasis in calf nutrition. He is studying how bioactive proteins can be used in the diet of preweaned calves.

Reproductive physiology research at UNH has focused on the improving conception rates and breeding efficiency of dairy cattle. Scientists D.H. Townson and P.C. Tsang are studying the function of the corpus luteum and how cows fall into two categories based on follicular waves.

The University of New Hampshire continues its research efforts to help dairy producers in the state and region. With the development of an organic dairy research farm, UNH is the first land-grant university to have an organic dairy. The goal of this dairy is two fold; first, to conduct research to determine the best cropping scenario for northeast dairy producers and second, to be a model organic dairy for our region's producers.

The NH Veterinary Diagnostic Laboratory is located at UNH and is under the supervision of J. Moore. It tests milk for mastitis organisms and performs autopsies on animals which have died due to disease. This assists farmers and veterinarians in diagnosing and controlling diseases on New Hampshire dairy farms.

It is apparent that the University of New Hampshire has a committed research emphasis to benefit our state's producers. This effort continues to this day. A new dairy nutrition research center has been constructed to continue this effort, adjacent to the Fairchild Dairy Teaching and Research Center.

Dairy Teaching

A major mission of the land-grant system is to educate the state's citizens and a major mission from the outset of this university has been to educate current and future dairy producers.

The dairy program at UNH has always had a presence. Beginning in 1992, the university developed a unique program

The old sheep barn in Lee, NH, has been converted to a milking parlor, holding area and maternity pens for the organic dairy.

The step-up parlor accommodates four cows at a time and lessens the bending required by the operator to milk the cows.

UNH Dairy Nutrition Research Center in Durham, NH.

to educate the next generation of dairy producers. With the help of the state's producers, the faculty within the Animal and Nutritional Sciences department developed a new major leading to a Bachelor of Science degree in Dairy Management, which combined applied dairy courses, traditional biology and business applications.

Recently, a new development between the Thompson School and the Animal and Nutritional Sciences Department allows students to transfer directly from the Associate's degree program into the B.S. program as a junior. Current professors teaching in the program include Conroy, Erickson and Schwab. There are active judging teams and a dairy club. Teams compete regularly at Eastern States exposition and occasionally at World Dairy Expo.

Dairy Extension

While Cooperative Extension in many states has been brushed by the wayside, the importance of the outreach arm of UNH to the state is apparent every day through the efforts of the state's dairy specialists. Past dairy specialists have included H. Boynton, T. Fairchild (who later went on to serve as Dean and later President of the university), J. Piwowar, J. Smith, R. Cady, and A. Young at the Durham campus. John Porter, a state dairy specialist located in a county office, played a major role in Cooperative Extension across the state. Farmers have looked to him for his expertise in barn design and family relations, and he has continued on a part-time basis after his retirement. He has published a book that has received national recognition on preserving old barns, along with former Agricultural Engineer Francis Gilman.

The Extension team of John Porter and Michal Lunak, Dairy Specialists, and Agricultural Economist, Mike Scibarassi, have worked tirelessly to educate dairy producers on best management and business development. Another major emphasis has been the development of a Johne's eradication program and biosecurity education for producers. This has been a collaborative effort between UNH Cooperative Extension (Erickson and Porter) and the state veterinarian. An award-winning educational video for new dairy hires was developed through cooperation of the Boston-based Walker Trust, UNH Cooperative Extension and the UNH Media Services office.

The University of New Hampshire continues to serve the dairy producers of our state through outreach, research and teaching. This continues the tradition set forth by Ben Thompson in his will that resulted in the University of New Hampshire being housed at Durham, "to promote the cause of agriculture wherein shall be thoroughly taught both in the school and in the field, the theory and practice of the most useful and honorable calling."

A Cooperative Extension meeting to educate area farmers, circa 1940s.

Farms are considering robotic milking. These units are located in the barn area and cows enter on their own to be milked. Shown above is a robotic unit at Nordic Farm, Shelburne, VT.

The Future of New Hampshire's Dairy Industry

New Hampshire dairy farm numbers have stabilized in recent years, and the industry will continue to have a presence in the future. The last bastion of the dairy industry will probably be along the Connecticut River Valley on the west side of the state. This is the area of some of the most fertile soils in the state and many land parcels have been preserved by easements or are in the flood plain. This area is also on the Vermont border, which makes the agricultural services of a larger dairy state available.

Looking into a crystal ball, future trends in the dairy industry might include:

- Return of milk production leadership to the traditional areas of the upper Midwest and Northeast due to water restrictions in the West and Southwest, energy concerns and transportation costs.

- Reversal of the trend toward mega dairies (1,000 plus cows) due to concerns about environmental pollution and requirements to own a designated amount of land per cow to dispose of animal wastes.

- Adoption of robotics for milking cows. This is a developing technology that won't go untapped by the dairy industry. Farmers replacing existing milking systems may find it economical to shift to robotic milking to save labor. This also lends itself to smaller farms, as animals need to be housed in 60-cow groups to be better served by a robotic milking unit. The first unit was installed in the fall of 2007 by Gordon and Nancy Gray of Graymist Farm in Groveton, NH.

- Reduction of concentrate (grain) feeding in dairy cow rations due to the competition for grains for human consumption and the genetic development of forages high in energy and protein content.

- Adoption of new housing designs for cattle to control odor, contain gases and improve foot health, such as the composted bedded pack which is currently being introduced.

- Increased use of rotational grazing, due to high petroleum costs, so cows can harvest their own feed part of the year instead of having it mechanically harvested.

- Use of specialized, contracted field harvesting services.

- Improvements made in small-scale methane gas generation from animal manure, encouraging the co-location of animal and plant-raising facilities to use the excess energy production.

The organic dairy herd is rotationally grazed on the pastures at the Burley-Demeritt Farm in Lee, NH.

- Development of modular construction components which can be made available to the dairy industry for quick on-site construction of dairy housing and milking facilities.

- Increased use of bio-diesel manufactured from waste cooking oil or oil-seed crops.

- Discoveries in human nutrition and the use of milk components in industrial manufacturing may cause an increased demand for milk production.

- Production of efficient, cost-effective, small-scale equipment will promote on-farm processing of dairy products to fill niche markets.

- Growing impact of agri-businesses in supplying information and consultation services to the dairy industry, but the University will still be looked on as a source of non-biased, research-based information.

- Increased recognition of the value of purchasing local food to help support New Hampshire agriculture and maintain open space.

The dairy industry will continue to be a viable industry made up of producers who are skilled in business management, nutrition, agronomy, animal health and mechanics, always ready to adopt the latest technology to remain competitive.

Gordon and Nancy Gray of Graymist Farm in Groveton, NH, were the first dairy producers in the state to install a robotic milking system. It is pictured under construction and went into operation in November, 2007. It is a DeLaval VMS (Voluntary Milking System) and is controlled by a computer. The cows are enticed into the machine two or three times a day by fresh feedings of grain and are identified upon entry. The robot sanitizes the udder before and after milking, attaches the milker unit, removes the unit when milking is complete and washes the equipment automatically several times during the day with no human intervention. The farmer's time is redirected from the milking chore routine to monitoring each cow's performance in the robot from computer printouts and checking the operation of the equipment. One machine can handle 65-70 cows and the total cost of all of the equipment involved in the operation is about $200,000, excluding the cost of the specialized building.

References

Achieving Smart Growth in New Hampshire. (2003, April). New Hampshire Office of State Planning.

Ad Hoc Associates for Squam Lake Association (1994). Property Tax and Development in the Squam Lake Area: 1990.

Adams, R. S., et al (1995). Dairy Reference Manual. Northeast Regional Agricultural Engineering Service. Cornell University, Ithaca, N.Y.

Auger, P. (1996). Does Open Space Pay? UNH Cooperative Extension.

Barnhart, G, R. (1947). The Development of Licenses and Order Regulating the Handling of Milk in Greater Boston, Massachusetts Marketing Area, November 3, 1933 – June 1, 1946. Unpublished dissertation on file with Department of Agriculture and Harvard University.

Bachelder, N.J. (1909). New Hampshire Farms for Summer Homes. The State Board of Agriculture, Concord, N.H.

Blayney, D.P. (2002). The Changing Landscape of U.S. Milk Production. USDA Statistical Bulletin No. 978.

Blayney, D.P. & Manchester, A.C. (2001). Milk Pricing in the United States. Economic Research Service, Agricultural Information Bulletin No. (AIB761).

Business Wire. (1997, August 25). Vermont Cabot Creamery – First U.S. Cheese Maker to Export Cheddar for Sale in England.

Chichilnisky, G. & Heal, G. (1998). Economic Returns from the Biosphere. Nature, Vol. 391, February, 629-630.

Chite, R. M. (1999, July). Provisions CRS Report 98-478 Agricultural in the FY 1998 Emergency Supplemental Appropriations Act (P.L. 105-174). Available at: http://digital.library.unt.edu/govdocs/crs/permalink/meta-crs-840:1.

Clark, R.H., Jr. (2006). New Hampshire Milk Bottles.

Coleman, J., et al. (2004, May). Conditions of Competition for Milk Protein Products in the U.S. Market. Publication No. 3692. Investigation No.: 332-453.

Collins, K. (2006, July 20). Testimony to Committee on Agriculture, Nutrition and Forestry. United States Senate. http://www.usda.gov/oce/newsroom/congressional_testing/Dairy%20Testimony7-20-2006.pdf.

Collins, W.M. (1987). NH Ag. Experiment Station. A History of the New Hampshire Agricultural Experiment Station 1887-1987.

The Cost of Community Services (2005). Town of Lee, New Hampshire. Lee Agricultural Committee.

Costanza, R. (2006). Toward an Ecological Economy. The Futurist, July-August, 26.

Czech, B. (2002). Technological Progress and Biodiversity Conservation: A Dollar Spent, a Dollar Burned. Conservation Biology, Vol. 17, No. 5, October, 1455-1457.

Dairyman. (1917, May).

Dasgupta, P., et. al. (2000). Economic Pathways to Ecological Sustainability. Bioscience, Vol. 50, April 339-349.

Davis, L. M. (1917). A Survey of the Dairy Marketing Conditions and Methods in New Hampshire. New Hampshire College Extension Service. Extension Bulletin No. 8.

Day, L. (2006, May 31). Prepared statement before the House Committee on Agriculture Subcommittee on Department Operations, Oversight, Dairy, Nutrition and Forestry.

Drake, D. & Grande, J. (2002). Assessment of Wildlife Depredation to Agricultural Crops in New Jersey. Extension Journal, Vol. 40, No. 1.

Dryer, J. (2007, Mar. 2). Dairy & Food Market Analyst, Vol. 14, No. 34.

Dublin, T. (1996, February). Transforming Women's Work: New England Lives in the Industrial Revolution. The American Historical Review, Vol. 101, No. 1.

Duffey, P. (2000, June). Making its mark Agri-Mark, New England's largest dairy cooperative, is building markets for producers USDA Rural Development. http://www.rurdev.usda.gov/rbs/pub/june00/Making.htm

Farmshine. (2007, August 10). Opposition to forward contracting noted. p.13.

Federal Milk Market Administrator Northeast Order Uniform Price for July 2007 Press Release. (2007, August 14).

Federal Milk Marketing Order Pooling, Depooling and Distant Pooling: Issues and Impact. (June, 2004). Paper No. 85. http://www.aae.wisc.edu/pubs/mpbpapers/pdf/mpb85.pdf.

Federal Order (2005). Northeast Market Area, General Provisions of Federal Milk Marketing Orders.

Foote, R. J. (1947, August). Wartime Dairy Policies. Journal of Farm Economics. Vol. 129, No. 3, pp. 679-690.

French, H.F. (1865). Agricultural Colleges. Department of Agriculture Report – 1865. Washington Government Printing Office, pp. 137-186.

Futurecasts. (2001, April 1). Descent Into the Depths (1930): Collapse of Agriculture. <u>Vol. 3</u>, No. 4. http://www.futurecasts.com/Depression_descent-end-'30.htm.

Galen, C. (2001, January 7). National Milk Producers Press Release.

Goss, L.E. (2003). The Impact of Agriculture on New Hampshire's Economy in Fiscal Year 2002. Institute for New Hampshire Studies. Plymouth State College.

Granite State Dairymen (1884 - 1998). Minutes of Granite State Dairymen's Association.

Hayes, D. (2004). Deflating the Ecological Bubble. <u>Conservation Biology, Vol. 18</u>, No. 6, December 1461-1462.

Implan Professional. (2004). Version 2.0 User's Guide, 3rd Edition.

Jacobson, R. & Wasserman, W. (1992, August). Regional Milk Bargaining Agencies and Cooperative Milk Price Bargaining. This paper is part of a series entitled "Dairy Markets and Policy – Issues and Options," a project of Cornell University's Program on Dairy Markets and Policy, pp. 1-5.

Jesse, E. & Cropp, R. (2004, January). Basic Milk Pricing Concepts for Dairy Farmers. University of Wisconsin Cooperative Extension publication A 3379. http://www.aae.wisc.edu/future/default.htm.

Judkins, H. F. & Keener, H. A. (1960). <u>Milk Production and Processing</u>. John Wiley & Sons, Inc., New York, London and Sydney.

LaFrance, J. T. (2003, September 16). The Economics of the U.S. Dairy Program Lecture Notes. http://are.berkeley.edu/courses/EEP141/fall2004/lecture_notes/Dairy-Program.pdf.

Lee, D. R. & Boisvert, R. N. (1985). <u>Factors Affecting Participation in the Milk Diversion Program in the U.S. and New York.</u>

Ludington, D. & Weeks, S. (2006). Digester Technology Works for a Smaller Herd. <u>Northeast Dairy Business</u>. East Syracuse, N.Y.

Manchester, A. C. & Blayney, D. P. (1997). The Structure of Dairy Markets: Past, Present, Future. Economic Research Service. USDA Agricultural Economic Report No 757.

Manchester, A. (1983). "The Public Role in the Dairy Economy: Why and How Governments Intervene in the Milk Business." Westview Press, Boulder, CO.

Market Administrator's Annual Statistical Bulletin Northeast Milk Marketing Area. (2001-2006). Federal Order No.1.

Market Administrators Bulletin Northeast Market Area. (2007, January). Federal Number 1. http://www.fmmone.com/Northeast_Order/Bulletin.

Market Administrators Bulletin Northeast Market Area. (2006, February 2). Federal Number 2. http://www.fmmone.com/Northeast_Order/MA_Bulletin/bull0602.pdf.

Moyer, J. N. (2003). From Dairy to Doorstep: The Processing and Sale of New Hampshire Dairy Products, 1860s to 1960s. Historical New Hampshire, Vol. 58, No. 3 & 4, pp. 101-122.

National Agricultural Statistics Service (1925-2006). Milk Production, Disposition and Income Annual Summaries.

National Agricultural Statistics Service (1970 - 2007). Milk Cows by Size Groups: Operations; Cattle and Calves. Cattle Inventory; Milk Production, Milk cows, Milk per cow: Annual.

National Agricultural Statistics Service (NASS), N.E. Annual Bulletins (1991 - 2006).

Natural Resources, Agriculture and Engineering Services (NRAES). (1988). Milking Systems and Milking Management, NRAES - 26. Ithaca, NY.

New England Farmer. (1943, September 6).

New Hampshire Changing Landscape. (2005). Society for the Protection of New Hampshire Forests.

New Hampshire Department of Agriculture, Markets & Food. http://www.agriculture.nh.gov.

New Hampshire Department of Agriculture Reports. (1879-1968).

New Hampshire Department of Health and Human Services, Division of Public Health Services (2005). Dairy Sanitation Program. List of Dairy Farms under permit.

New Hampshire Housing Finance Authority. (2005). Housing and School Enrollment in New Hampshire: An Expanded View. Prepared by Applied Economic Research.

Newton, I. (1865). Report of the Commissioner of Agriculture. Department of Agriculture Report 1865. Washington Government Printing Office. pp. 1-11.

Nickens, E. (1988). A Watershed Paradox. American Forests, Vol. 103, Issue 4, 21-24.

Northeast Farm Summary. (2000 - 2006). A Joint Project of Northeast Farm Credit.

Oehler, J. (2005). Social Impacts of Dairy Farming and Wildlife. Email correspondence.

Porter, C.H. (1985). Agriculture Past and Present. Grange Presentation.

Porter, J.C. and Gilman, F.E. (2001). Preserving Old Barns. UNH Press.

Reifer, S. (2001, April). Greener Acres, Vegetarian Times, pp. 67-72.

Resource Systems Group. (1999). The Economic Impact of Open Space in New Hampshire. The Society for the Protection of New Hampshire Forests.

Ring, W. (2001). Farm Bill Restructures Dairy Subsidy Program. http://www.fmpc.uconn.edu/research/compact/ring.pdf.

Rivlin, A. M. (1979, April 11). Statement before the U.S. House of Representatives. Dairy and Poultry Subcommittee of the Committee on Agriculture.

Roadhouse, C. L. & Henderson, J. L. (1950). The Market-Milk Industry, McGraw-Hill Book Company, Inc., New York.

Selitzer, R. (1976). The Dairy Industry in America. Dairy Field, New York.

Shapiro, L. & Kroll, H. (2003, June). Estimates of Select Economic Values of New Hampshire Lakes, Rivers, Streams and Ponds. Gallagher, Callahan & Gartrell, P.A. Concord, N.H.

Short, S. D. (1989, Jan-March). National Food Review. http://findarticles.com/p/articles/mi_m3284/is_n1_v12/ai_7678617.

State of New Hampshire, Reports of State Board of Health. (1924-1939).

Taylor, D. (2000). Groton Cost of Community Services Study. New Hampshire Wildlife Federation.

Trust for Public Land. (2005). Managing Growth: the Impact of Conservation and Development on Property Taxes in New Hampshire.

Tscharntke, T., et al. (2005). Landscape Perspectives on Agricultural Intensification and Biodiversity – Ecosystem Management. Ecology Letter, Vol. 8, pp. 857-874.

U.S. Census of Agriculture. 1850, 1860, 1870, 1880, 1890, 1900. Census Reports of the United States Agriculture.

U.S. Census of Agriculture (1950). General Report. Volume II.

U.S. Census of Agriculture (1970). Historical Statistics of the United States, Colonial Times to 1970.

U.S. Census of Agriculture, N.H. (2002, June). USDA.

United States Code. (2006). Title 7 of Agricultural Chapter 26 – Agricultural Adjustment Subchapter I – Declaration of Conditions and Policy Section 602 – Declaration of policy; establishment of price basing period; marketing standards; orderly supply flow; circumstances.

USDA/AMS Dairy Programs, Washington, DC. (2002, October 31). Study of the Dairy Forward Pricing Pilot Program and Its Effect on Prices Paid Producers for Milk. p. 5. http://www.ams.usda.gov/Dairy/for_contr/report_no_appendices.pdf.

USDA Economic Effects of U.S. Dairy Policy and Alternative Approaches to Milk Pricing. (2004, July).

USDA Economic Research Service (2000). A History of Agriculture, 1607-2000.

USDA, Farm Service Agency. Milk Income Loss Contract Program. Fact Sheet: Electronic Edition. http://www.fsa.usda.gov/.

U.S. Imports of Concentrated Milk Proteins: What We Know and Don't Know. (2003, February). Market and Policy Briefing Paper 80. Dept. of Agricultural and Applied Economics, University of Wisconsin-Madison.

U.S. Soil Conservation Service, N.H. Department of Agriculture Association of Conservation Districts, N.H. Conservation Committee and UNH College of Life Sciences and Agriculture (1976). 200 Years on the Land. Bicentennial publication.

Walski, T.W. (2005). New Hampshire Wild Turkey Assessment. N.H. Fish and Game Department.

Weld, I.C. (1905). The Dairy Industry in New Hampshire. New Hampshire College Agricultural Experiment Station. Bulletin 120.

Wellington, R. (2006, April). Speaker at the Agri-Mark Dairy Cooperative Meeting.

Weisbecker, A. (2007, April). A Legal History of Raw Milking in the United States. <u>Journal of Environmental Health</u>.

Whitaker, G.M. (1905). The Milk Supply of Boston, New York and Philadelphia. U.S. Department of Agriculture, Bureau of Animal Industry. Bulletin 81.

World Book Encyclopedia.

Appendix

Appendix A - Calculating the Minnesota-Wisconsin (M-W) Price

To calculate the M-W monthly price, two surveys were mailed to Grade B milk processors that produced butter, nonfat dry milk and cheese in the Minnesota and Wisconsin areas. The first survey requested the amount of dollars paid, volume and butterfat of the raw milk purchased. This information helped calculate the base month price. Another survey sent to a smaller sample of milk processors determined the prices paid during the first two weeks of the current month and any expected change in the prices they were paying for the last two weeks of the month. The monthly M-W price was calculated using the base month price, the results from the second survey, and additional information such as historical price and manufactured dairy product prices. Once calculated, the price was announced by the fifth day of the month following production.

Appendix B - Changes in Milk Pricing Formulas

Changes in Milk Pricing

Basic Formula Price 1995	MCP/PPD Jan. 1, 2000
Class I price = Class III or Basic Formula Price (national price) + Class I differential (order specific)	Class I price = higher of Class III price (national price) or Class IV price (national price) + Class I differential (order specific)
Class II price = Basic Formula Price + $0.30/cwt (national)	Class II price = Class IV price (national price) + $0.70/cwt (national)
Class III or BFP (national) Minnesota-Wisconsin Grade B price updated by a product price formula	Class III price (national) Formula based on butter, cheese, and whey prices
Class III-A (national) Formula based on nonfat dry milk prices and the butterfat differential	Class IV price (national) Formula based on butter and nonfat dry milk prices

Appendix C - Understanding Milk Classes and Pricing

To arrive at values, the National Agricultural Statistics Service (NASS) conducts weekly surveys of sale prices and volume traded of Cheddar cheese (40-lb. block and 500-lb. barrel styles), butter, nonfat dry milk, and dry whey from manufacturers that meet NASS's reporting criteria. Then using specified formulas, the Agricultural Marketing Service determines the value of each component based on the results of either two-week or monthly (the most recent four or five-week period) averages of dairy product prices and yield allowances. In setting prices, each class of products relies on a different mix of the survey prices.

Class I milk includes all fluid or beverage milk that contains more than 6.5 percent nonfat milk solids or greater than 2.25 percent true protein and less than 9.0 percent milk fat. Skim milk, flavored milks, eggnog and buttermilk are also considered Class I products. Since the Federal Order regulations are written to assure an adequate supply of beverage-eligible milk, the final Class I price is adjusted by a county differential reflecting the location of the plant that processes the milk.

For the Northeast Order, the pricing point is Suffolk County (Boston, MA) and the differential ranges from $2.10 to $3.25 per hundred pounds. Generally, the differential increases from west to east and from north to south relative to the Upper Midwest region and reflects the percentage of milk in the Order used for drinking purposes, with orders using a higher percent of milk as fluid or beverage milk receiving higher Class I prices. While the differential doesn't prevent milk produced from other areas from competing with local milk, it protects farmers against the price fluctuations that would occur if a dealer who has surplus milk is willing to sell it at any price.

The minimum for Class I price is an "advance" price allowing a milk dealer to know before he prices his milk how much the milk will cost him. The price is equal to the higher of the advanced Class III or Class IV skim milk prices and the Class I butterfat price as determined by two weeks of NASS survey data for cheese, whey, butter and non-fat dry milk conducted during the month the figures are released. According to the Northeast Federal Milk Market Order, 44.6 percent of the nearly 2 billion pounds of milk produced in May, 2007, was used for fluid products. Milk used to manufacture Class III products such as cheese (American and Italian) and evaporated and condensed products use 22.8 percent of total milk receipts. Class IV usage (butter, nonfat and whole milk powder) equaled 10.8 percent of the total.

Class II milk products continue to be classified as those usually consumed with a spoon including ice cream, yogurt, sour cream, cream cheese (previously a Class III product) and cottage cheese. Products that contain a high amount of milk fat (i.e. whipping cream and half and half) also fall into this category and use approximately 22 percent of the milk produced (Federal Milk Market Office, June 2007).

The Class II prices are determined by a formula that uses both butterfat and nonfat solids prices, derived from NASS survey prices of butter and nonfat dry milk prices (NFDM) with the resulting price equal to the Class IV price plus 70 cents. The Class IV price is sometimes higher than the Class II price under this formula, because NASS survey prices are from different weeks with the advanced skim milk price announced before production occurs, but the butterfat price, another component value of the Class II, not announced until the fifth day of the month following production or approximately 42 days after the advanced price is announced. This formula represents a major change from the previous program that priced Class II products mainly on cheese prices plus a specific Class II differential.

Class III and Class IV milk products are usually referred to as hard products because they can be stored for longer periods of time. Class III products include cheese (American, Cheddar, and Italian) and uses 22.8 percent of total milk receipts while Class IV products including butter, nonfat and whole milk powder and evaporated or sweetened condensed uses 10.8 percent of the production (Federal Milk Market Office, June, 2007).

The Class III and IV component values are determined based on the results of a formula that uses four or five NASS mandatory surveys. For the Class III price, butter, cheddar cheese and dry whey prices are used to compute values for butterfat, protein, and other solids, respectively. The protein and other solids prices are used to calculate the Class III skim milk price that, combined with the butterfat price, determine the Class III milk price. While the nonfat solids price is used to calculate the Class IV skim milk price that combined with the butterfat price, determines the Class IV milk price. The Class II, III, and IV prices are the same in each Federal Milk Order and are announced by the fifth of the following month.

Pool Announcement with Line Explanation

To further understand these concepts, look at the May, 2007, Pool Price Announcement accessed at: http://www.fmmone.com/Northeast_Order_Prices/Uniform_prices/up0705.pdf

United States Department of Agriculture Agricultural Marketing Service Dairy Programs

FEDERAL MILK ORDER
No. 1
Northeast Marketing Area

89 South Street, Boston MA 02111-2671
Mailing Address
P.O. Box 51478 Boston, MA 02205-1478
Tel.: (617) 737-7199 — Fax: (617) 737-8002
email: MABoston@fedmilk1.com
website: www.fmmone.com

Albany: 302A Washington Avenue Ext. Albany, NY 12203-7303 Tel.: (518) 452-4410 Fax: (518) 464-6468 email: MAAlbany@fedmilk1.com Alexandria: P.O. Box 25828 Alexandria, VA 22313-5828 Tel.: (703) 549-7000 Fax: (703) 549-7003 email: MAAlexandria@fedmilk1.com

MAY 2007
POOL PRICE ANNOUNCEMENT

1.

Producer Milk	Percent	Pounds	Minimum Class Price
Class I	44.6	887,595,430	$19.17
Class II	21.8	434,025,163	16.62
Class III	22.8	453,715,557	17.60
Class IV Total Producer Milk	10.8	213,424,005	18.48
	100.0	1,988,760,155	

3. Computation of Uniform Price (per cwt @ Suffolk County, MA - Boston)
Producer Price Differential
Class III Price (@ 3.5% Butterfat)
Statistical Uniform Price (@ 3.5% Butterfat)
Statistical Uniform Price (@ Average Pool Component Tests)

2. Class III & Producer Component Prices

Protein Price $2.9424 /lb
Butterfat Price 1.5706 /lb
Other Solids Price 0.5791 /lb
Nonfat Solids Price 1.4949 /lb

4. COMPUTATION OF PRODUCER PRICE DIFFERENTIAL

	Product Pounds	Price per cwt./lb	Component Value	Total Value
Class I— Skim	870,867,825	$ 14.53	126,537,094.97	
Butterfat	16,727,605	1.4714	24,612,998.00	
Less: Location Adjustment to Handlers			(2,817,216.01)	$148,332,876.98
Class II— Butterfat, 486	30,146,486	1.5776	47,559,096.30	
Nonfat Solids	36,572,086	1.2778	46,731,811.50	94,290,907.80
Class III— Butterfat	16,703,611	1.5706	26,234,691.41	
Protein	13,670,430	2.9424	40,223,873.26	
Other Solids	25,908,234	0.5791	15,003,458.32	81,462,022.99
Class IV— Butterfat	8,631,016	1.5706	13,555,873.73	
Nonfat Solids	18,521,133	1.4949	27,687,241.74	41,243,115.47

Total Classified Value	**$365,328,923.24**
Add: Overage—All Classes	76,010.82
Inventory Reclassification—All Classes	394,615.55
Other Source Receipts 11,407 Pounds	195.72
5. Total Pool Value	**$365,799,745.33**
6. Less: Producer Component Valuations @ Class III Component Prices	(355,443,391.21)
7. Total PPD Value Before Adjustments	**$10,356,354.12**
Add: Location Adjustment to Producers	9,582,811.39
One-half Unobligated Balance—Producer Settlement Fund	851,508.56
Less: Producer Settlement Fund—Reserve	(902,958.37)
Total Pool Milk & PPD Value 1,988,771,562 Producer pounds	**$19,887,715.70**

8. Producer Price Differential $1.00

Statistical Uniform Price $18.60

Explanation:

No. 1 - Is the percentage of milk used in each class, the pounds of milk that this represents and the federal order minimum price that was established for each hundred pounds for the class.

No. 2 - To determine the Class lll and Producer Component Prices the individual component prices are determined by multiplying each of the components in milk by the price per pound of which results in the total component value. These figures when added together equal the total pool value. The Class lll and component prices consist of the protein; butterfat, other solids and nonfat solids determined from NASS surveys

No. 3 - Is the result of the calculations to determine the Uniform Price, the Producer Price Differential, the Class III announced price for milk that is at 3.5 percent butterfat, the Statistical Uniform Price (comparable to blend price) at 3.5 percent and the price that the average farmer receives.

No. 4 - Is determining the PPD. We find that the total classified value of all milk marketed in the pool is $365,328,923.24

No. 5 - Some adjustments are made to this number to determine the total pool value of $365,799,745.33.

No. 6 - From the amount in number 5, the amount that the farmers will receive for the components or Class III values is deducted.

No. 7 - Is the total PPD that is the value of milk in the pool beyond the Class III component values identified in number 6. Adjustments that the order regulations require are then made to this number. The PPD is calculated and announced for the base city in a federal order and is then "adjusted" to each of the plants located throughout the order. The adjustments to the PPD are equal to the relative differences in the Class I differential.

No. 8 - When the total producer pounds of milk are divided into the number listed in number 8, the result is the PPD, which when added to the announced Class III price results in the Statistical Uniform Price.

Appendix D – Producer Settlement Fund

Dealers or Processors Obligation to the Producer Settlement Fund:

Class I   Class I skim milk price at location x skim milk pounds.

Class I butterfat price at location x butterfat pounds.

Class II   Class II nonfat solids price x nonfat solids pounds.

Class II butterfat price x butterfat pounds.

Class III Protein price x protein pounds.

Other solids price x other solids pounds.

Butterfat price x butterfat pounds.

Class IV Nonfat Solids price x nonfat solids pounds.

Butterfat price x butterfat pounds.

Appendix E – Understanding Your Milk Check

Using "Bob the farmer" to illustrate, let's see how these numbers work. Bob shipped 50,000 pounds of milk during the month of May that tested 3.90% butterfat, 3.15% protein, and 5.66% other solids. Bob's milk check is going to be based on the Market Administrator Butterfat price of $1.5706 per pound, Protein Price of $2.9424 per pound, and other solids price of $0.5791 per pound and a PPD at Suffolk County, MA, of $1.00 per hundred pounds.

Category:	Price:	Pounds:	Value:
3.90% butterfat times	Butterfat price $1.5706 /lb times	50,000 pounds	$3,062.67
3.15% protein times	Protein price $2.9424 times	50,000 pounds	$4,634.28
5.66% Other Solids times	OS price $0.5791 times	50,000 pounds	$163.88
---------------------	----------------------	Components =	$7,860.83
Federal Order PPD	PPD/cwt of $1.00 times	500.00 CWT =	$500.00
Minimum Obligation at	Suffolk County, MA =	---------	$8,360.83

In the above example, the farmer receives a minimum of approximately $16.72 for each 100 pounds of milk he produces plus any premiums minus any deductions.

Appendix F – Location Differentials

Producer Price Differential and Statistical Uniform Price, by Location[1]

Selected Locations	Differential*	Adjustment	Producer Price Differential (Dollars per cwt)	# Stat. Uniform Price
Boston, MA	3.25	0.00	1.00	18.60
Albany/Binghamton, NY	2.70	(0.55)	0.45	18.05
Middlebury, VT	2.60	(0.65)	0.35	17.95
Syracuse, NY	2.50	(0.75)	0.25	17.85
St. Albans/Swanton, VT	2.40	(0.85)	0.15	17.75

* Differentials listed apply to states included in the Northeast marketing area. Outside of this area, differentials and prices may be above or below this range. Cities listed are for reference purposes only.

\# Prices apply on a county basis. Prices at 3.5 percent butterfat, 2.99 percent protein, and 5.69 percent other solids.

(Footnote)

[1] http://www.fmmone.com/Northeast_Order_Prices/Uniform_prices/up0705.pdf

Appendix G – Synopsis of What Federal Milk Marketing Orders Do and Do Not Do

Federal Orders:

- Ensure farmers are paid accurately for the milk they produce. This is done by verifying bulk tank calibrations and component tests from the milk samples the milk hauler takes at the farm for farmers who don't receive the service from a cooperative.

- Ensure farmers are paid for their milk on a timely basis using at least the minimum price announced by the Market Administrator monthly.

- Set minimum prices for milk according to how it is used.

- Regulate processors and those who collect milk from the farm at the point milk is processed by requiring them to accurately report the amount of milk they receive and how that milk is used monthly so classification can take place.

- Require all processors to pay their producers. The Market Administrator's office also develops market information and statistical summaries and publishes records on the number of producers, the amount of milk produced and the use of milk for each Federal Order. (This information can be accessed through the FMMO website at www.fmmone.com.)

- Investigate any complaints of violations of the Order.

Federal Orders Do Not:

- Guarantee a fixed price to producers, regulate the volume of milk dairy farmers can sell or guarantee a market for a producer's milk. Producers must find their own market and must arrange for the delivery of their milk to the milk dealer.

- Determine the maximum price farmers receive for their milk. Farmers can negotiate premiums for milk that meet certain standards.

- Establish sanitary or quality standards (state governments and cooperatives do this).

- Regulate trade at the wholesale or retail level. The Market Administrator can't regulate the price retailers charge for milk or the percentage of profit they make on milk.

- Prevent payments at an amount higher than the minimum established by the Market Administrator.

- Prohibit milk from being marketed anywhere in the United States.

- Have authority to regulate who processing plants can buy from or sell to, how much milk the plant can buy or sell or the price the milk processor sells his or her milk to a retailer.

Information supplied by Federal Milk Marketing Order One.